Mastering
NINTENDO®
Video Games

Judd Robbins
and
Joshua Robbins

HAYDEN BOOKS
A Division of Howard W. Sams & Company
4300 West 62nd Street
Indianapolis, Indiana 46268 USA

FIRST EDITION
FIRST PRINTING—1989

International Standard Book Number:
0-672-48464-2
Library of Congress Catalog Card Number:
89-62989

Acquisitions Editor: *James S. Hill*
Development Editor: *James Rounds*
Manuscript Editor: *Don MacLaren, BooksCraft, Inc.*
Production Coordinator: *Kathy Ewing*
Illustrator: *Don Clemons*
Icon Designer: *Dean Johnson Design, Inc.*
Cover Artist: *Tim Amrhein*
Compositor: *Typoservice*

Printed in the United States of America

Trademark Acknowledgments

CONTENTS

Part

Part

Turbo Tips, 137

Part

123

Mini Tips and Game Summaries, 149

ALPHABETICAL LIST OF GAMES

GAMES BY CATEGORY

Arcade Category:

Arcade Category (cont.)

Action Category:

Sports:

Adventure:

GAMES BY MANUFACTURER

ACKNOWLEDGMENTS

Thanks to all of those companies that donated game cartridges during the research for this book: Jaleco USA, Inc; Tradewest; LJN Toys; HAL America.

And thanks, also, to those companies that sent us information, rules, hints and tips, and game maps: Jaleco, American Sammy, Broderbund, Mattel, Capcom, Acclaim, Mindscape.

Thanks to Jim Hill of Howard W. Sams & Company for the original idea to do this book.

Last, but certainly not least, we'd like to thank all of the kids that contributed tips, drawings, and game counseling (playing!). We'd like to thank Eli Robbins for game tips and tricks and for helping to pry tips out of his friends (not an easy task). Special thanks to the following kids for great tips: Jacob Rosenbaum, Patrick Petzel, Matt Brown, Jae Yi, Daniel Bodvarsson, Douglas Friedmutter, Joseph McDonald, Sasha Peterson, Jonathan Vlahos, and Gabe Marshank. Extra special thanks to Josh's fresh buddies from the KSG and members of the three Amigos: Jonathan Vlahos and Sasha Peterson; "LANBBAM." Thank you all.

INTRODUCTION

Welcome to *Mastering Nintendo Video Games,* the best source around for finding the Number 1 tips, tricks, and techniques. This book is designed to help kids of *all* age groups master all of the best tricks in the book (this book, that is!). The large print and appealing layout make it easy to quickly find your favorite game and get the answers you've been looking for.

The book has been written from the point of view of a child. It is meant to be easily understood by the young readers most interested in mastering the fun games presented.

In Part 1, Mega Reviews, look for the *Power Tips:* these are the best tips and codes for each game. You can find still more hot tips by flipping to Part 2, which includes Turbo Tips: the hottest passwords and secret features—one or two per game. Part 3, Mini Tips, gives still more tips, plus game summaries.

The Mega Review section contains extensive information about 24 of the most popular games around. It is based on a highest possible rating in each Category of 4.0 and is organized as follows:

1) Rating

Overall rating: How good is this game, in our opinion?

Challenge: Can you win this game after one evening, or does its challenging play last a long time?

Sound and Graphics: How good are the graphics, and how realistic are the sound effects?

 The highest possible rating for each category is 4.0. The best of the games are marked with this icon.

2) Story

What the game is all about and, usually, what has to be accomplished in the game before winning.

3) Main Characters

A list of the main characters, either played by you, or against you. This section tells of their strengths and weaknesses, and of the weapons they use.

4) Hints

This is the main section of the book. It includes the tricks, tips, and techniques that can make you the best player on your block.

 ## 5) Power Tips

These tips are marked with this icon and are the best hints you can imagine! These tips are usually secret passwords, secret Continue features, extra life opportunities, and level-select features.

Once you have finished reading this book, you should have almost no questions left about these Nintendo video games, because you'll already know even more than you ever dreamed of knowing.

For best results, read this book from cover to cover, then memorize it, and recite it to your best friend. Thanks for buying the key to winning all of your favorite Nintendo games.

123

Mega Reviews:
In-Depth Closeups

ADVENTURES OF LOLO

 Overall Rating = 3.5
Challenge = 4
Sound and Graphics = 3

Story

This game takes place in Eden, a once-peaceful land that had everything anyone could ever want. One day the Great Devil of Destruction came and ruined everything. He destroyed the fields of flowers and took over all of Eden.

The King of Eden sent his daughter, Lala, to the Great God of Eden to ask for help in defeating the Great Devil of Destruction. The Great God told Prince Lolo to journey with Lala to the castle of the Great Devil. Unfortunately, the Great Devil learned of this plan, and he kidnapped Lala and brought her to his castle.

To rescue Lala, you, as Lolo, must fight your way through 10 dangerous floors with 5 rooms on each floor. On each floor, you must solve a puzzle. Each new puzzle is harder than the last. You must find a way to collect all the heart framers on the screen and capture the treasure. The only help that the Great God of Eden can give is this commandment: *"Never put two shots into the river of the underworld!"* If you disobey this commandment, you won't be able to use a password, a Continue, or to press SELECT in order to kill yourself.

Main Characters

LOLO—The trustworthy Prince who is on a mission to rescue Lala from the Great Devil of Destruction.

LALA—The King of Eden's daughter who was kidnapped by the Great Devil.

SKULLS—These monsters seem to be dead, but once you have picked up all of the heart framers on the screen, they will come after you.

DONMEDOSA—If you cross his eyesights, he will kill you.

MEDOSA—He will do exactly the same thing as Donmedosa.

ROCKY—He will move slowly around the screen, but when he is face to face with Lolo, he will charge and try to trap you.

LEEVA—He will run around the screen, but if you touch him, he will be paralyzed for life.

GOLL—He throws a flame at Lolo after you have taken all of the heart framers.

SNAKY—He is your only friend in this huge castle. Snaky will let you turn him into an egg and move him to block fire thrown by the monsters.

General Tips

Plan Ahead

When you enter a room for the first time, stop and think for a while. Look at the setup of the room, the enemies you have to deal with, and how many helpful items (emerald or heart framers) or friends (Snakies) are on the screen. Plan how you are going to go about solving the puzzle and then try your plan.

Egg Raft

In room 2 on the third floor, you'll have to use an egg as a raft. Put the egg in the water, get on, jump across to the heart, jump back on the egg and then quickly off the egg over to the treasure chest. It is tricky, but try it with this password: *BRBD*.

No Fair—They're Cheating!

Yes, it's true, monsters do cheat. None of your shots can go through trees, rocks, or hearts, but the monsters *can* shoot through trees.

Think First

Always think before you make a move. Don't move an emerald framer against a wall unless you know you won't need it for anything else. Don't put a bridge in the water unless you are sure that it is the correct place.

The rest of the hints and tips are for the all-important last room of each of the floors.

Floor 1, Room 5 (Password = BHBP*)*

When you first enter this room—don't move! Study the room. Once you move, the Rockies will run after you and you won't be able to stop until you get all of the hearts and the treasure. Start off by moving straight up. The Rockies will pass you, so you have time to get the upper-left heart. Next, go for the lower-right heart. Turn quickly to fake out the Rockies and get the upper-right heart by pushing the emerald all the way in. Finally, lure the Rockies to the top and scoot to the lower-left corner to claim the last heart and get the treasure. Be careful—don't go for a heart if a Rocky is close to you.

Floor 2, Room 5 (Password = BPBH*)*

First, get the two heart framers at the top of the screen. You now have two magic shots. Use one shot on the Alma in the lower-left corner of the screen and push him against the left wall and up until he is blocking the bottom of the Skull. Next, you want the heart in the corner—but don't try to capture it yet! First, use your power to change the direction of the arrow. Push the second emerald from the top all the way left against the wall and now get the heart on the left. Carefully bring the top emerald out and use it to block the other side of the Skull blocked by the Alma. Now go back through the arrow and push the original block up to the corner. Then push the second block from the bottom left once, up once, right twice, and up and out to block the upper-left Skull. Finally, block the last Skull by turning the Snaky into an egg and then get the heart. Phew!

Floor 3, Room 5 (Password = BYZZ)

This room is not difficult to get through. Stop reading here if you think you can figure this one out! First, get the two hearts to the right of the treasure chest and the three on the top half of the screen. Next, get the heart touching the left wall and the next-to-last heart on the bottom left. Finally, push the emerald framer down three notches, to the right two spaces, down once, and then right until it is between the pink guy and the last heart. Get the heart and *roll!*

Floor 4, Room 5 (Password = CGZO)

Begin by going up the screen, pushing the left emerald to block the pink monster's fire while you get the heart. Turn one of the Snakies into an egg and push him left and up so that he is blocking the pink guy who would fire at you from the top. Then use the other Snaky to block the other guy from firing on the top. Take the heart at the top center of the screen and come down. Get the last heart in the upper-left corner and come down for the chest. Simple!

Floor 5, Room 5 (Password = CMZJ)

Start by moving up and making a quick left so that you are at the top of three arrows in a row. Go down until you reach the rock at the bottom. Move right until you reach the first arrow. Quickly go up and make a sharp right until you hit the wall. Push the framer all the way down and then go left until you hit a rock. Quickly move up left and then down without touching any framers. Move left two spaces so that you are under the left arrow. Move up to the rock and then left and push the framer all the way up to the rock. Get the heart and go back the way you came until you're under a heart framer and an emerald framer. Push the emerald framer up until it is blocking the right side of the purple face. Return to get the heart in the upper-left corner of the screen. Go right until you are on a right arrow. Go down and hang a sharp right until you get to a right arrow. Go up, then right to the heart. Go down and push the second-from-the-top framer to the right. Finally, push the framer down, right, and all the way up. Phew!

Floor 6, Room 5 (Password = CVZB)

You must work extremely fast in this room. First, get the heart framer and then shoot the Snaky and push him into the water. Ride on the Snaky until you are next to the emerald framer and push left so that the framer is blocking the purple face from below. Run over and push the other emerald framer to the right and then UP so that it is blocking your enemy from the left side. As the egg floats into the channel, use it as a bridge to get the two hearts on the island and then hop back on the egg and float on it all the way around to the treasure chest.

Floor 7, Room 5 (Password = DDYR)

This one is fairly simple. Check out the green grass inside the skull area. The Skulls cannot travel on the grass. There are eight Skulls, and you only need one framer to block every two Skulls. Get three of the four hearts on the outside, and use power to change the top right arrow. Notice where the hearts are located. Get the two hearts on the top and slide the top-right and bottom-right framers into the positions where the hearts were. Repeat these moves on the left side, except this time use your power to change the bottom-left arrow. Once you have blocked all of the Skulls, get the last heart and go in for the treasure chest.

Floor 8, Room 5 (Password = DLYK*)*

Don't get the heart right below you yet! Instead, go to the upper-left corner and get that heart. Then get the heart in the middle at the top and push down the emerald that is above the down arrow. Push it out to the bush—don't let the pink monsters see you!—and push it to the right until it is below the heart we told you not to touch. Now, get that heart and push the framer down to trap the enemy. Next, go all the way back to the upper-left corner and push the framer on the right down, but stop before you get to the arrow. Push the framer to the left of you (on top) to the left until it hits the rock. Get above it and push it down and trap the second pink monster exactly as you did the first one. Now you should have three framers in a row near the top and a lone framer. Push the middle framer up one block and push the left one to the left. Now push the left one down and out through the arrow. Put it above the purple face and get the heart. Now go through the upper-left arrow and push the framer to the right so that it is above the rock. Go down, then right, then up, and push the framer left so that it is above the down arrow. Bring it down and out to block the other side of the purple enemy. Repeat these steps, using the other two blocks against the other purple guy. Then get the heart in the upper-right corner, grab the chest, and climb the stairs!

Floor 9, Room 5 (Password = DTYC*)*

Don't get the heart on the bottom-right yet! Instead, push the bottom-right framer up one block so that it is blocking the purple monster. Then get the lower of the two hearts in the middle and push the framer it was above up to block the purple guy. Get the heart to your right and push the framer on the far right up one block. Push up 2½ notches the framer that was above the last heart you picked up. The framer should be partly blocking the second highest purple monster. Adjust the framer just enough up from the bottom so that the purple guy can't shoot. Now push the framer that is between the pink and purple enemies toward the purple. Finally, push the framer that is above you up to block the other purple monster. Push it as high as you can so that it is still blocking the enemy and you have a passageway to the treasure. Now go back down, get the heart, and *run nonstop* up to the treasure chest.

Floor 10, Room 5 (Password = GCVT)

This one took us a while to figure out. First read this and memorize what you are going to do. Go up and get the heart. Run over to the door and shoot down so that the top-left monster is an egg. Run over to stand on the down arrow and then shoot down. Move left, then down, and push the egg right. Go left, up, right two spaces, and push the egg all the way down to the bottom. You must do all of that before the egg cracks. Then go to the top, between the two bridges. Run to the bottom and make a sharp right turn for the treasure. If you're fast enough, it will work, because all of the enemy shots will miss you. Go out the door for an ending that is pretty spectacular!

More Passwords

These are the answers to 10 out of 50 of the puzzles in this game. If you are having trouble with a particular level, here are 9 more codes for the *first* room of each level: *BJBM—BQBG—BZZY—CHZP—CPZH—CYYZ—DGYQ—DMYJ—DVYB.*

AMAGON

Overall rating = 2.5
Challenge = 3
Sound and Graphics = 2

Story

The courageous soldier, Amagon, is on a mission to investigate an island that nobody has ever returned from. He must travel through six zones—the Island, the Jungle, the Rivers, Rain Forests, Mountains, and the Beach—and avoid tarantulas, bats, alligators, and other dangerous enemies. Although he is only armed with a machine gun, he also has a special power that allows him to transform into Megagon, a megastrong, super-powered man.

Main Characters

AMAGON—The brave soldier who must investigate an island full of perils.

TARANTULAS—These large spiders want you dead!

VAMPIRE BATS—They want to suck your blood!

ALLIGATORS—They come onto land and try to eat you alive. They can shoot from their mouths.

PTERODACTYLS—These enemies fly in the sky and swoop down to try to eat you.

PURPLE FROGS—These unfriendly frogs shoot lasers out of their mouths if you get too close to them.

UFOs—Unidentified flying objects that can kill you easily.

LIONHEAD—One of the enemies at the end of each zone, Lionhead appears to be just a big head of a lion, but it is really *two* lion heads.

DEVIL TREE—Another enemy that appears at the end of a level.

HIPPO DEMON—This demon is really a big blue hippo head that just gives off a lot of smoke.

Hints

Help

In the beginning of zone 2, you will have to cross the river on top of a turtle. You will be attacked by porcupines and bees, but if you duck and just keep shooting over and over again, you should be fine.

Danger!

Just after the location of the 1-UP sign, you will have to cross a river. Be ready to use your gun on your first jump. Start shooting *as you jump* in order to get rid of the bird that appears.

10,000-Point Bonus

Right after the tree with the 1-UP symbol, a bird will swoop down again and again. If you want to add 10,000 points to your score, just sit and shoot this bird over and over, because sooner or later, it will be carrying a crown with your bonus.

Megagon

Save your Megagon strength—only turn into Megagon at the end of each level. You don't really need the power any other time, but you *will* need it to defeat the monster at the end of each level.

Purple Frogs

Kill these colorful frogs by standing at a distance and firing your machine gun. Don't try to run up close to them and attack them, because they will blast you with a laser.

Secret 1-UP

About halfway through zone 1-2, you'll come to an area with a tree in between rock formations. Stand up on the rocks to the left and shoot the tarantula in the tree. Quickly hop onto the rocks on the right and then jump up to get the 1-UP.

Defeat Alligators

When an Alligator walks toward you, he will spit a wad of bullets from his mouth. The trick to defeating him is to lie on the ground and fire away. Keep firing, though, because you have to hit him 16 times before he gives up. This trick also works for Elephants.

Bullets

Right after you leave the area with the darting birds in zone 1-2, you come to an area with many tarantulas, most of which carry bullet magazines. Take advantage of this opportunity to get as many bullets as possible.

Avoid the Deadly Bird

After the tarantula-bullet party we just described, there will be a big dropoff. Be alert—a bird will come out of nowhere once you have jumped down to the first island. Position yourself about 2 inches from the edge of the cliff. As you land, press the jump button continually. The timing will be just right so that you hop right over the deadly bird.

Mosquitos

Right at the start of zone 2-1, a group of mosquitos will fly toward you. Shooting them will gain you some bullets, but for best results, shoot them when they are flying in a group.

Elephant Man Tip

When the Elephant Man moves to the right, he runs and fires faster than when he is moving to the left.

Ditch Elephant Man

When the Elephant Man comes at you in zone 2-1, jump up on the branch on the far left side of the screen and move to the farthest left point on the branch. From this position, you can watch the overgrown elephant walk right off the screen!

Devil Tree Tip

When you encounter the Devil Tree, shoot only at its eyes. This is the only area where you can injure him.

Defeat WASPS

Here's a little trick to help you defeat the wasps. Jump high up in the air to make a wasp shoot high and then stoop down low to the ground and wait for the wasp to shoot its bullet above you. Then get up and shoot the wasp.

Continuation Feature

Once you get to zone 4, you will have earned the continuation feature, which enables you to start on any level of the game. However, if you decide to venture back to zones 1, 2, or 3 and then you die before you make it back to zone 4, you will not be able to continue.

Hot Stuff!

Right at the start of zone 2-2, there will be a bunch of moles. Kill them and they'll give you many important items. Keep destroying them until they stop giving stuff.

Mega Bullets

In zone 3-1, you will see some snails at the waterfall. Shoot them. Don't pass them up, for if you shoot them, they'll give you many extra bullets.

Defeat the Hippo Demon

At the end of zone 3-2, you will be faced with the challenge of fighting the Hippo Demon. Make sure that all of your shots are aimed toward its nose (right under the eyes). Keep firing at those nostrils until the whole enemy is destroyed.

More Extra Bullets

At the beginning of zone 4, you will encounter many spirits spinning toward you. *Do not* pass up these spirits, because they'll give you lots of bullets which you'll need to finish the game.

BIONIC COMMANDO

Overall rating = 3
Challenge = 3.5
Sound and Graphics = 2.5

Story

Super Joe is being held captive in a hidden prison by the Imperial Army. You have been chosen to rescue him. You must also find out the secret of the Albatros plan. To win, you must cross over beaches, deserts, and finally blow up a hidden underground lab. At the start, you are armed only with your bionic arm, which is an extendable arm with a grappling hook at the end. You can win weapons throughout the game, but you can also lose them through battles. You must also find soldiers who are kind enough to give you helpful information.

Main Characters

SOLDIERS—These enemies come at you with machine guns.

CYBORG GENERAL—A super-powerful bionic creature that is 51% robot and 49% human. He has *triple* the amount of your bionic strength!

SUPER JOE—He is the man that you must save. Once he is rescued, he will give you a bundle of important information.

CRANE—This is a moving vehicle with a driver in it. You'll need two shots of a rocket launcher to defeat it.

VENUS FLYTRAPS—Their name says it all! These are the famous fly-eating plants, but now they have been trained to eat you too!

Hints

Get a Continue

The name of this object is misleading, because it is really an extra man. You can get a Continue after you have killed the last enemy of each stage.

Use Your Helmet

If you're in an area that is loaded with enemies, it's a good time to use your helmet. With the helmet on, the next three enemy bullets will bounce right off you. The helmet is in a secret passage described in the next power tip.

Hidden Passages

To find out where the hidden passages are, find a room in area 17 that has a man on the other side of a spiked ditch. Use your bionic skills to cross the pit, and then the man will talk to you. Once you've done that, all of the hidden passages will be shown on your map.

Blow Up the Core

Destroying the core is usually a difficult thing because soldiers keep coming and coming. If you stand on the same level as the core, directly under the far right edge of the platform above you, you can shoot the core all you like and the soldiers won't be able to hurt you!

Explore

On each level, you must go in every door and you must kill every enemy, look at everything, and use your time wisely in the correspondence rooms. Sometimes, you can't advance to the next stage unless you have finished the one before it.

Swing That Arm!

You can use your bionic arm to climb up walls, swing over barrels, swing across open space, and even to snatch things that enemies have left behind. It can also prove useful to dodge enemies.

When wading in the water on the beach level, you can swing your Grappling Hook Arm around your head like a lasso. This technique is especially useful when you are being attacked from all sides.

Fly Over Obstacles

At some time during the game, you will encounter a barrier that you cannot destroy because you don't have the Rocket Launcher. An easy way to pass this place is to press A, B, and START all at the same time. You will rise up and fly off the screen!

Doors

Make sure that you enter *every single door,* because lots of times, you will find valuable information or even weapons you can use.

Shoot the Barrier

A barrier is in the 15th neutral zone. Shoot this barrier right away and hurry to a doorway to collect a useful item. But be careful, for neutral zones turn into battle areas right after you start firing your guns.

Get the Machine Gun

We can't tell you exactly where to get the machine gun, but Super Joe can—once you save him. When you get where he says to go, there will be three men offering you the machine gun. The first two are phony, but the third one is the real thing.

Invincible Man

You can't destroy the last man at the end of the desert, who is guarding some sort of an opening. You can try every weapon you have against him, but none will work. You must *go around* him.

Bionic Weapon

If you get in a jam, with an enemy flying above you, you can still kill it. For example, in area 3, a large insect flies right over you. Your bullets can only go left and right, but you can still use your bionic arm to kill the fly.

Avoid a Level

When you get to level 8, you have a choice of levels to try. Since level 8 is extremely hard, skip it to do better in the game.

BUBBLE BOBBLE

Overall Rating = 2.5

Challenge = 3.5

Sound and Graphics = 1.5

Story

Two brontosaurus pals, Bub and Bob, have had their two best buddies kidnapped by the terrible Baron von Blubba. They now are determined to venture to the Baron's land to find their lost friends. Little do they know that von Blubba has sent out thousands of small monsters to stop Bub and Bob from getting to the palace. The dinosaurs must travel through 226 rooms to find their friends, and their only weapon for fighting the monsters is the amazing ability to blow huge bubbles around their enemies and pop them, leaving no trace of the enemy. This is a long game, and one that uses passwords. If you use the codes we reveal here your life will be a lot easier.

Main Characters

BUB and BOB—They are the stars of the show. They can blow bubbles around their enemies, making them defenseless.

INCENDO—He is a very difficult enemy to defeat. Incendo will spit fire at you, so be careful.

WHALES—These enemies are easiest to destroy, for they are easily lured into your bubbles.

SUPER SOCKET—He is a real meany!! Watch out or he'll spit on you.

COILEY—He can annoy you with his hops, skips, and jumps.

BUBBLE BUSTER—There's not much to say about this guy—except that his name is his game!

GRUMPLE GROMMIT—He is one mean sucker! The Grommit will spit bubble after bubble *at you,* and boy, is he tough.

BARON VON BLUBBA—This enemy is bubble-proof, and he will come and kill you if you spend too much time on any level. For instance, on levels past 80, you only have about 10 seconds before you are Blubba meat.

Hints

Line 'em Up!

Here's a nifty trick that will help you move fast and increase your points quickly. Blow a whole bunch of bubbles around a few enemies and line them up. Get at the end of the line and push. They'll fall like dominoes!

Bubble Ride

Try different ways to use your bubble-blowing ability. For instance, a neat trick is to blow a bubble and hop on it. In this way, you can hitch a ride up to a level you couldn't otherwise access.

Ending Code

Here is a secret code that will bring you to the last level of the first BUBBLE BOBBLE quest: *E E C J J.* Here is the code that will bring you to the last level of the entire game, just before the final duel of SUPER BUBBLE BOBBLE: *E E C F G.*

Don't Make the First Move

When you are battling the Baron's monsters, it is best to wait until they attack you before trying to kill them. If you go after them first, they'll swarm all over you. If you let them attack you, they won't attack in such large numbers.

Beluga Tactics

The Beluga fish are rough and tough. They will swallow you in one gulp if you don't get them in a bubble first. The easiest way to defeat these Belugas is to have some help: a second player. When you get into a room with Belugas, use the following power trick to bring in a second player.

Player 2, Come on Down!

Any time during the game, you can bring in a second player to help you. Press A and B at the same time you press the SELECT button. It is very important that you use this trick when you are battling the final Boss, because if you do not win with two players, you'll get a *bad end,* instead of a *happy end.*

Level 99 Clue

Once you pass level 99 on the game's first quest, you will be given a clue that will help you win the game. If you can't wait 99 levels, the password is *G E J F J.*

Defeat Grumple Grommit

Using the password, *HJFAB,* go to the level F5. You'll have about 2 seconds before the Grumple Grommit comes to life to eat you. Jog to the left and get the Drug of Thunder and then go to the bottom of the screen. It's best if you have Slo-Mo on your NES Advantage or Max, but if you don't, just try hard. Run to the far left side and hide in the corner while shooting at the Grommit. When he gets near, run to the opposite side and repeat these moves. Keep doing this (remember to stay in the corners!) until the Grumple Grommit is dead.

Challenge Yourself

If you really want to work yourself to the max, use these passwords for more advanced levels:

96—*GGJBI*

89—*CAJFI*

F5—*HJFAB.*

Secret Passwords

Since our favorite number is four, we'll reveal passwords for a few screens that have the number 4 in them.

Level 1, Screen 43—*IEJJJ*

Level 2, Screen 4—*BIBEG*

Level 2, Screen 14—*BECIJ.*

CASTLEVANIA II: SIMON'S QUEST

 Overall Rating = 3
Challenge = 4
Sound and Graphics = 2

Story

Simon's mission is to find the last five missing parts of Count Dracula: The ring, the nail, the rib bone, the eye, and the heart. Simon must fight zombies and other monsters to get hearts and clues. He must journey through towns, woods, marshes, and mansions before he can get to the Castlevania castle. Good Luck!

Main Characters

SIMON—You control Simon. He can get five different whips and hold a lot of utilities.

OLD FOLKS—These elders can give you friendly advice that will help you later in the game.

ZOMBIES—Zombies only roam around at night. They don't want to talk to you; they want to kill you. If you kill them first, you will receive hearts that you can use as money.

THE GRIM REAPER—This enemy floats around holding a long blade. You must kill him with the fire whip to get the Golden Knife.

COUNT DRACULA—The well-known caped man is hiding in Castlevania. He is the last character in the game that you will have to face.

Hints

Raw Password

Use this password to start the game with the morning star, fire bombs, holy water, dagger, red crystal, Dracula's rib bone, two laurels, and two garlics: *REJ5 DYV0 GG8F XTRT.*

Fire Bomb

In the Aljiba woods, there is a screen with three levels of stairs. You can destroy the first level by throwing the holy water at both of the bricks. Move Simon left until there is a dead end. Use your holy water on the wall to reveal the fire weapon. Wow!

Talk, Talk, Talk

Make sure that you talk to every man or woman in all of the towns, because they all hold important information.

Invisible Elevator

Just inside the entrance to the Berkeley Mansion, you'll come to a dead end. To reveal the invisible elevator, press SELECT to choose one of your crystals. The elevator will appear and you can proceed.

Buy Garlic and Laurel

When you are in a town and offered a sale of laurel or garlic, *buy it!* The laurel makes you invincible, which is terrific, and the garlic has the power to freeze enemies in their tracks for a while.

Oak Stake—A Must!

If you forget to buy the oak stake from the old man, you will be in trouble. You must have the oak stake in order to obtain all the parts of Dracula.

 Password for Aljiba Woods

Use Dracula's eye right after you punch in this code: *7MTM QXFV 1X4J XQJ5.*

Ride the Ferry

When you are on the ferry crossing the dead river, talk to him, for he will tell you a lot. If you are holding Dracula's heart while you are talking to him, he will bring you to Brahms' Mansion.

Cross the Poison Swamp

To cross the swamp in the Belasco Marsh, you must hold on to the rib bone and jump up and down while making the crossing. It helps tremendously if you have the laurel that you bought earlier.

Underwater Secret

At some point, you will encounter a dead end where you can only go into the water. A secret lies under the water here. Hold up your crystal while kneeling down and press button A. The water will rise up, revealing a secret passageway.

Clues in Brahms' Mansion

Two clues are hidden inside the Brahms' Mansion. The first clue is about where you can get the silk bag, and the second clue tells of Deborah Cliff's secret.

The Best Password

This password will start you off with everything—yes, *everything*—possible that you can get in the game. Here it is: *CT6D QZ6K RXXN VTRK*. Your next job is to find Castlevania.

Secrets in Rooms

Usually, when you enter a room that has a man in it, a secret door will be on the far right. Just throw your holy water at the wall to reveal the opening.

Spoil the Ferryman

When you are invited onto a ferry for a lift, you might be taken some place that you don't want to go. To avoid this, offer the ferryman some garlic. He will then take you to a good place.

Skeleton Ride

Have you ever ridden a skeleton? You can, if you want. When the skeleton attacks you, and there isn't enough room to swing your whip, just jump up on its head! You won't be injured, and you won't have to fight the skeleton.

Veros Village Hints

The first time you go through the village of Veros, you will not get many items or obtain much information. But if you go through the whole Berkeley Mansion and then go back to Veros for a second time, there will be more people to give you clues and items.

Empty Shop?

If you enter a shop and there is nobody in it, a secret passage is usually hidden there. Look at the ground and at the far right wall. Throw your holy water at these two places, and a secret may be revealed.

Graveyard Clue

When you get to the Camilla Cemetary, try all sorts of things using your items on the fourth gravestone, and soon an important puzzle piece will appear.

DEADLY TOWERS

Overall Rating = 3.5

Challenge = 4

Sound and Graphics = 3

Story

Prince Myer, the son of the King of Willner, is going to be promoted to King soon and he wants nothing to get in his way. Unfortunately, Rubas, the Prince of Darkness, doesn't want Myer to become King. Rubas is preparing to invade the Willner Palace. To do this, he must go to all seven of his magic Bell Towers and collect an army of monsters to help with his evil plans. Prince Myer's quest is to find all seven bell towers and burn them. Once that is done, he will become king and everybody will live happily ever after.

Main Characters

These are the names of all of the different enemies that you will encounter throughout the game.

BOUNDERS, CLONES, DEVILS, DRAGONS, FIRE BEINGS, FISH BEINGS, GHOSTS, HUMANOID MONSTERS, INSECT BEINGS, RAT BEINGS, SLIME BEINGS, SNAKES, TOWER BOSSES

Hints

Entrance to Dungeon 1

The entrance to the first dungeon is not a visible door, but rather a sort of teleport. To get there, go to the right at the start of the game. Keep going until you are stopped by a dead end and a pillar. Face the pillar and you will be teleported to the first dungeon.

The following shops are shown on the map in Figure DT1:

1. Red Drink, Shield, Figure
2. Red Drink, Glove, Orange Necklace
3. Red Drink, Shield, Red Crystal
4. Red Drink, Short Sword, Chain Helmet

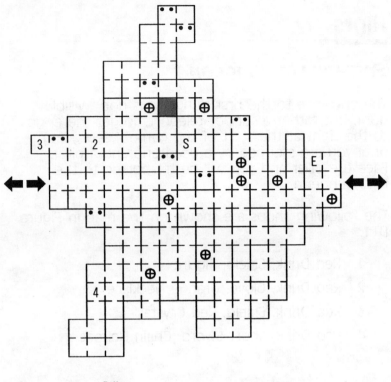

• • = Pillars
S = Start
E = Exit

Figure DT1. Map of First Dungeon

Hidden Store

There is a secret hidden shop not far from the beginning of the game. To get there, go to the right and up through the first door that you see. Go to the right, along the narrow passageway and make sure you don't get knocked off. Go in the door and then move to the top of the screen. You will be magically teleported to a shop that sells fire magic for 60 ludder, red drink for 30 ludder, and chain helmets for 80 ludders each.

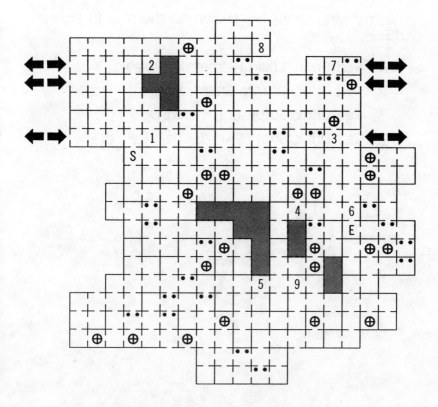

Figure DT2. Map of Second Dungeon

Dungeon 3 Info

To get to the entrance to the third dungeon, go up in the first door that you see and then immediately go up through the next door. Then go left to the second door and go up in it. Kill the dragon and go through its door. Then move to the right until you see two statues in the wall and a door to their right. Go in the door and move left until you see a door. *Do not* go in this door, but instead move yourself to the lower-left corner of the screen. Move around a little and you will be warped to Dungeon 3.

The following shops are shown on the map in Figure DT3:

1. Red Drink, Chain Helmet, Fire Magic
2. Red Drink, Bronze Shield, Figure
3. Red Drink, Surprise 1, Expensive 2
4. Red Drink, Short Sword, Chain Helmet

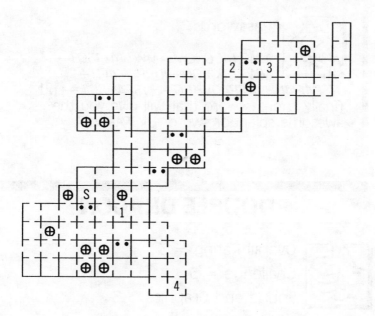

Figure DT3. Map of Third Dungeon

Mega Weapons

To start your game with all level 3 defense and attack items (dragon-slayer sword, gauntlet glove, hyper helmet, king's shield, and hyper armor), you must use this little trick on your pass code. Start off your game and die immediately. Then change the first digit of your pass code to an E. Then make the second digit an F. Press start and you will have only the best weaponry.

Hit Point Fill Up

If you find that you are a little low on Hit Points after you beat one of the bosses, do this: Take the bell that you got from the boss and bring it to the holy flame and burn it. All your hit points will be given back.

Passwords

*MWTT4COPQM—MWTT4Z15QJ—
MWTT4KX.QN—IURP4PI4FH—
JTSP4PI4HH-JTSP4QVHHG—HVSP4NGGIL—*and
finally, the password that will give you the
awesome splendor sword: *HVSPAPIVYZ.*

DOUBLE DRAGON

Overall Rating = 3
Challenge = 3
Sound and Graphics = 3

Story

Billy Lee and his twin brother, Jimmy Lee, are two
karate fighters who are on a mission to save Billy's
girlfriend, Marian, from the Shadow Boss. His gang,
the Black Warriors, have kidnapped Marian, and Billy
and Jimmy must go through four tough missions
before they meet face to face with the Shadow Boss.
They must fight many strong men who don't want
them to get to the Shadow Boss.

Main Characters

BILLY AND JIMMY—These two characters are controlled
by you. As they gain hearts, they can make better
moves like spin kicks, hair pull kicks, and head butts.
But what they can do, when they do it, and who they
do it to, is all up to you.

LINDA—She is a feisty little character who will come at you with a whip. Without her whip, though, she can be easily beaten.

LOPAR—This man comes at you with punches and kicks and sometimes throws a barrel of oil at you. Be careful!

WILLIAMS—He is easily destroyed with a jump kick. Sometimes he carries a baseball bat, and if you knock him down, the bat is yours.

CHINTAI—This man is an expert in karate. He knows how to do jump kicks and he also likes to trip you.

ABOBO—Abobo lives in a cave, and he is extremely strong. He can bash through walls, and he will probably bash through you!

SHADOW BOSS—The main evil guy who is holding Billy's girlfriend captive. His abilities will remain a secret!

Hints

Earn Hearts

The more hearts you have, the trickier moves you can make. One trick is to kick an enemy once or twice, let him recover, kick him once or twice again, let him regain his strength, and do it a whole bunch more times. Don't knock him down until at least the fourth or fifth time. It takes a little longer overall, but this trick gives you many points, which give you hearts quickly.

Easy-Out Boss Room

Mission 1: Stand on the blue conveyor belt and lure the enemies onto it. Make sure you are on their *left* so that when you knock them down, you can watch them fall right over the edge to their doom.

Block the Knife

On mission 3, when a man approaches you with a knife, you can block his throw. Just before he throws it at you, press A and B at the same time to perform a jump kick. Now you can pick up the knife and throw it at him!

Dodge Boxes and Barrels

When your enemy approaches you with a box, barrel, or knife in his hand, there is an easy way to dodge it. Let him get close to you until he begins the motion to throw his item. Immediately dodge either up or down. Then go and pick up the thrown weapon and fight fire with fire!

Hearts the Easy Way

Right at the beginning of the second mission, you'll see a pile of orange steel bars. Position yourself as high up on the screen as you can and start to punch and kick the area where one bar is sticking out until you hit an invisible man. Watch your hearts start to multiply! But beware, it doesn't always work.

Ditch Chintai

At the end of mission 2, at the top of the stairs, Chintai is waiting to beat you up. You don't even have to put up a fight—just climb down the ladder until Chintai is pushed off the screen. Climb down the next ladder, and about halfway down the ladder, you will freeze and the level will be passed.

Abobo's Cave

On mission 3, if you miss the entrance to Abobo's cave, you could get caught in a loop forever. When Abobo crashes through the wall, he leaves a hole. Try going in the hole. If you don't get in, you will never pass level 3. Remember, you have to knock down both Abobos *first*.

Awesome Weapon

In mission 4, you must beat up the Chintais. Let the knife that one of them has drop to the ground and pick it up right after the last Chintai blinks for the fourth time. This weapon looks like a club. To make it even better, you can kill all the Lindas with it. Near the end of the fight, let a Linda knock it out of your hands. Kill the last Linda and pick the club up again after her fourth blink. Awesome!

Chintai's Cave

As with Abobo's cave, if you miss the entrance, you'll be looped back to the beginning of the mission. The entrance to Chintai's cave is inside Abobo's cave. It is the first door on the right after you cross the moving platforms. Of course, you must beat the two Chintais first.

Ditch Abobo

On mission 4, there will be an Abobo waiting for you near a stony wall. When you see him approaching, climb the wall and watch him pass!

Cement Block Trick

For this technique, you must have incredibly good timing. When you get to the part where cement blocks come out of the walls, wait for the first block to come out twice. Immediately after that, make a wild run to the right, without stopping once. If you do it right, every stone block will just miss you.

GAUNTLET

Overall rating = 2.5

Challenge = 3

Sound and Graphics = 2

Story

Morak, the Evil One, has stolen the Sacred Orb. You (Thor) and your three friends—Thyra, Merlin, and Questor—are on a mission to steal back the Sacred Orb. There are over a hundred rooms between you and the Sacred Orb. Do you have what it takes to get back the Orb?

Main Characters

THOR—He knows no magic tricks, but he has an axe and is a big, strong man.

THYRA—She is the Valkyrie with a lot of strong armor. She has the speed and courage to fight the evil forces.

MERLIN—The wizard can do absolutely nothing but magic. He does it well, though.

QUESTOR—This elf is the fastest character in the game, and he fires his arrows with ease.

Hints

Food Sacrifices

When you are around food, be careful not to shoot it, for some food can be destroyed. It is the strength potions that can be destroyed, not the bowls of food.

Mega Passwords

Here are passwords for Thor and Thyra that will start them out about halfway through the entire game:

Thor—*BC3-SY9-ISS*

Thyra—*NRF-TTU-NR7*

Demons in Chests

Be awake when you open locked chests, because a black demon will be lying in some of them. Fortunately, most will hold treasures, potions, and exits.

41

Exit Room 9

In room 9, you will find that you are going around in a spiral to find the exit. The easiest way to the door is to just run around *counter-clockwise* and avoid all of the enemies.

Double Power!

Enter either one of the passwords given in the first power tip for both characters in a two-player game. The two will be exactly the same! Let one of them get killed and take all of that one's possessions for the other guy. He now has double the power.

Destroy Generators

If you ever want to get anywhere in this game, you must set your priorities straight. You should always destroy the enemy generators first, before you go for the ghosts or goblins, because if you don't, the ghosts and goblins will keep generating and attacking you.

Cooperation!

When playing a game with four or more people, take advantage of the different skills that each character has. For example, when there is a big crowd of ghosts, let Merlin stay back and perform his magic and Questor stay back to shoot his arrows while Thor and Thyra fight up front in hand-to-hand combat.

How to Continue

At the end of the game, when you see your password at the bottom of the screen, hold down the A button, press START, and let go of the A button. Wowee!

Ditch Enemies

If you are standing on one side of a closed door and a swarm of enemies is on the other side, try to make the enemies move for a second. When you move up, so do they! Try moving up quickly and then moving down and through the door for a clean getaway. This trick works best with Questor.

Share Items

When you come across a magic potion, let Merlin get it, because he is the most skilled at using magic. Also, let the character with the least amount of energy get the food when it comes around. Don't give the extra speed potion to Questor, because he is already fast enough.

Room 79 Codes

To start your game in room 79 with a hefty inventory, use these codes:

Merlin—*43C-BBI-HZY*

Questor—*43C-BBI-HYY*

Thyra—*43C-BBI-HYZ*

Thor—*43C-BBI-HZZ*

Get Clues

To get a clue in the clue room, you must find the ? sign. Do this by opening chests, touching trap doors, and shooting at and pushing walls. Don't forget to watch your time!

Don't Risk Life

If you see a whole lot of enemies near a whole lot of treasure chests, just turn up your nose and walk away. There is no need to risk losing some of your energy over points, because the important thing in the game is the level, not the points.

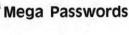

Mega Passwords

Here are the passwords for Merlin and Questor that will start them halfway through the game.

Merlin—*UTL-DST-LGT*

Questor—*77F-TA1-NLS*

Ditch Demons

When you see a black demon, *do not* go over to it and say, "What's up?" and then try to kill it. The only way to kill the demon is with magic, and Merlin is best at that. Just run up and away from the demon, and he will disappear in no time.

GOLGO 13: TOP SECRET EPISODE

Overall Rating = 3.5

Challenge = 4

Sound and Graphics = 3

Story

A helicopter that was carrying a deadly drug called Cassandra-G was blown up and the CIA thinks that Golgo 13 did it. A secret group called Fixer believes that Golgo 13 is not responsible, but rather that the sinister Drek empire is responsible. Fixer has hired Golgo 13 to find Drek and get back the drug. During his journey, Golgo 13 must seek information and clues as to the whereabouts of the Drek empire while fighting the CIA, KGB, and Drek.

You must travel in cities while visiting hotels, airports, buildings, and even train stations to find the necessary clues needed to complete your mission. When in the air, you must shoot down jets, missiles, and other helicopters in order to stay alive. You must travel through such well-known places as Berlin, Greece, and Antarctica. This game is a fast-paced action game and you must keep on your toes throughout.

Main Characters

GOLGO 13—Duke Togo used to work for the KGB, and now he is with Fixer. He must find the person responsible for the bombing of the helicopter or *he* will be blamed.

OZ WINDHAM—A Fixer who is being held hostage in Berlin by the Drek empire.

RED RIVER JR.—The Fixer messenger who carries important information for Golgo 13 throughout the game.

CHERRY GRACE—This good-looking woman is positioned near Drek's hideout in Berlin, and she gives Golgo 13 new weapons and secret information.

CONDOR—Condor has many secrets that would help Golgo 13 in his mission, but Condor will only tell these secrets if Golgo 13 acts fast and makes it to his hideout in time.

MOTORCYCLE WILLY—This is one of your enemies who will come at you while driving a motorcycle.

Hints

Rolling Thunder Truck

The first time you enter the stage that you fight in your helicopter, you will be attacked by a giant thing called the Rolling Thunder. The best thing to do is to fly way down at the bottom of the screen and fire continuously at the middle object as the fireballs hit you. You will almost definitely lose all of your energy, but as soon as you defeat the Rolling Thunder, you will get all of your energy back. Make sure that you have *at least* 30 rounds of ammo before you enter this stage.

Hot Clues

The hottest clues are almost always found in the subway stations, so make sure that you visit every single subway station.

Uh-Oh—Missiles!

Just as you switch to the action-packed pan and zoom screen, you will be faced with a couple of missiles and ships coming right at you. For safety reasons, shoot the missiles first and then the planes.

Extra Ammo: Life = Bullets

This trick only works when you are in the underground bases. It's actually very simple: If you need a bullet, press the SELECT button. Each time you press SELECT, one of your Life points will be transformed into a bullet. The only catch is that you can only do this 10 times.

Defeat Motorcycle Willy

Motorcycle Willy will drive straight at you while doing a wheelie. The trick to defeating him is to jump up and shoot him while you are in midair. If you can't do that, just use a jump kick. Please don't try this at home!

Order of Life (or Death)

When you switch to the pan and zoom screen, you will be faced with flying airplanes and with snipers on the ground. Your best bet is to go for the enemies on the ground first and then shoot at the planes.

Secret Stage Select

Wait until the demo game is done and a closeup picture of Golgo 13's eye is showing on the screen. On controller 1, press the START button. Let go of START and then press and hold the A button, the B button, and push UP on the control pad. On controller 2, press and hold the UP and LEFT diagonal while holding both the A and B buttons. While all of these buttons are being held, press START on controller 1. If 00 doesn't appear on the screen, try again. If 00 appears now, press either UP or DOWN to change the code to one of the codes in the chart. You'll move up to the act indicated.

Act	Code	Act	Code
1	00	5	1E
2	08	7	32
3	0A	9	3B
4	12	13	49

Ditch Planes

The planes are usually the hardest of all your enemies to defeat. Hover for a while to learn the patterns the planes fly before making a move. Sometimes the best thing to do is to fly between the planes. This uses the least energy.

Grenade Givers

The only people that will give you extra grenades are the men that are carrying machine guns. Shoot them and they will give you grenades.

Real or Fake Base?

Two bases are underwater in Berlin: a fake one and a real one. There is a way to identify these bases. The fake base has grey walls and is located in very shallow water. The real base is located in much deeper water and has blue walls. The entrance to the real base is just outside, once you go up the ladder.

Useful Maps

This game has a whole bunch of maps in the instruction manual. Make good use of these maps: mark the spots that you are in, the spots you have been in, and which direction you are facing. Also mark where the secret items are located and where the enemies are hidden.

Keep That Guard Up

Just like Mike Tyson, always keep your guard up. Also, keep your gun out when you are inside any of the bases. If you don't, you'll be caught off guard and blown back into the water.

Exit Greece to Aegean Sea

First, be sure to visit the hotel in Greece and then go just to the right of the Parthenon where two groups of trees and bushes are. Position yourself right in between the bushes and press UP. This will bring you just about to the Aegean Sea.

GRADIUS

Overall rating = 3

Challenge = 4

Sound and Graphics = 2

Story

The Bacterions, a fierce alien colony, are attacking Gradius. You must fly on your spaceship called the Warp Rattler until you get to Xaerous, the Bacterion hideout. Once there, you must destroy the fortress and the leader of the Bacterion gang. Your journey to their hideout will bring you through these eight stages: Space, Volcanic, Stonehenge, Inverted Volcanic, Moai, Antennoid, Amoeboid, and the Superfortress.

Main Characters

ANTENNOIDS—These aliens have long tentacles that help them fire their weapons at you. They fly through space with ease.

AMOEBOIDS—These aliens look more like the balls of slime used in Ghostbusters. If you get too close to them, you will be eaten.

JUMPER—A robot that patrols all of the ground bases.

DAKKER—A cannon that shoots at you from the ground.

DAI #01—This is also a cannon, but it has more power than the DAKKER.

RUGURR—A fighter plane.

ZAB—A land mine.

FOSS—An enemy ship.

TILD—A very small version of the attacking ships.

DAGOOM—A hanger for the enemy ships.

Hints

Secret Continue

To return to the last level that you were on, press the controller DOWN, UP, and then push B, A, B, A, B, A, B, A, and START.

Defeat the Brain

Here's a little trick to beating the Brain before it electrocutes you. Get way back to the left, exactly in the middle, and just shoot and shoot away. It will really help if you use the trick in the next power tip to gain rapid firing power.

Rapid Fire Replacement

To make your joystick into a *turbo firing machine,* destroy a whole bunch of enemies until you have six capsules and your indicator shows a ? mark. Keep getting points until the fourth digit from the right on your score is a 0. Once it is a zero, get a seventh capsule. Hold down the A button, and you will have Rapid Fire.

Stay Out of the Corner

If you are fighting from the left side of the screen, make sure that you stay in the center and don't drift up towards the corner. If you do, you might get trapped by ships, and you'll be very vulnerable to their shots.

10,000-Point Bonus

Collect six capsules until there is a ? mark on your indicator, and the fourth digit from the right on your score is a 5. Take one more capsule, and you will get a 10,000-point bonus!

Straight Away!

In the beginning of the game, you will have to go through the Space stage. It is real simple, because you don't have to do any work at all. Just go straight without touching the control pad. The only thing you should use is the A button because it will shoot your ammo. All of the Rugurrs will come to you and into your line of fire.

Warp, Warp, Warp!

In stage 1, when the thousands digit of your score is even, try to destroy four hatches in a row. Then defeat the core fighter, and you will warp to level 2. While warping, if you do not touch any of the Moais, you will warp to stage 3. In stage 3, kill 10 Moais, and after you beat the final enemy, you will warp to stage 5. Finally, to warp from stage 2 to stage 4, you have only 2 seconds to beat the Xaerous fighter while the core is blue.

Secret 1-UP

In stage 1, touch the back of your ship to the far right tip of the floating rock when the thousands digit is even.

5000-Point Bonus

In stage 1, steer your ship through the large crack in the volcano. You now have 5,000 extra points!

Mega Starship

If you would like to begin with missiles, one speed, two options, and a shield, do this: start the game, and then immediately pause the game. Press UP, UP, DOWN, DOWN, LEFT, RIGHT, LEFT, RIGHT, B, A. Then unpause the game.

HUDSON'S ADVENTURE ISLAND

Overall Rating = 2.5

Challenge = 3.5

Sound and Graphics = 2

Story

You play the role of Master Higgins, and you must rescue the Princess Leilani. She has been kidnapped by the Evil Witch Doctor and is being held captive somewhere on Adventure Island. The Evil Witch Doctor has set out all sorts of traps that you must overcome on your journey.

Main Characters

MASTER HIGGINS—Higgins is a little shrimp who can either run or skateboard. He can collect weapons like stone axes, fireballs, and honey girls.

STONES AND BOULDERS—These are dropped down on Higgins, and the only ways he can destroy them are with fireballs or with a honey girl.

OCTOPUSES—Blue Octopuses take two hits, but red ones only take one.

KELLOS—Green Kellos won't hurt you, but the brown ones sure will!

SNEIL and SKELETON—These are simple little critters that are only worth 10 points.

BIG KAHUNA—He is the boss at the end of each of the eight areas.

KING QUILLER—This is the last battle you will have to fight to win the game.

Hints

Caution—Eggplant!

On world 1-3, an eggplant is hiding inside an egg next to the third pillar. If you are curious—and foolish—and decide to pick up this egg after we give you fair warning, you'll pay the price! P.S. Right before this eggplant, there is also a hidden egg that holds fireballs.

Hidden Eggs

To find hidden eggs, you must jump in the right place at the right time. On world 1-2, eggs are usually hidden on ledges right at the ends of cliffs. The easiest way to find all of the hidden eggs is to jump straight up on every ledge before and after a cliff.

Secret Bonus Stage and Warp

On world 1-1, section 3, stand between the last two totem poles for about 3 seconds, and a magic cloud will appear and lift you up into the sky. Awesome!

Jump Higher

Did you know that if you run before you jump, you will jump higher than standing still and then jumping? Use this bit of info to get up to high places easily.

Find Secret Areas

On Hudson's Adventure Island there are many secret magical areas. These either contain a hidden egg or a bonus stage. To find out where these areas are, start throwing your axes *everywhere*. They will usually fall to the ground, but in a magic area they will disappear into thin air! When this happens, start jumping!

Fireballs

The second egg in world 1-1 is a skateboard. Start riding the board until you meet up with a bird. *Do not kill it!* Just skate right into it! You'll fall off your board with no injuries and an egg will appear. In it are fireballs.

Mega Bonus Points

When you see a running coyote, kill it! You'll get a whole bunch of bonus points.

Find Honey Girls

In round 1-1, right after all five totem poles, the first egg contains a honey girl. In round 1-2, when you touch land for the fourth time, there will be a palm tree. Keep going forward until you see a cloud and then land again. The egg on the edge here holds a Honey Girl.

Continue Forever!

Right before the end of 1-1, jump up and down in the area to the left of the goal sign. An egg that holds the Hudson Bee will appear. Get the bee, and when your game is over, hold the controller RIGHT and press START at the same time in order to continue playing.

Bonus Stage

On world 1-3, a bonus stage is hidden right after the red bricks. First, get the key out of the egg that is hidden on the edge of the bricks before the platform. Then get on the platform and wait for it to rise up to the sky and into the bonus stage.

Double Your Score

Sometime during each round there will be a bonus pot. Make sure that you get it, because it will double your score at the end of the round!

How to Kill Bosses

Position yourself very close to the boss and wait until he throws fireballs past you. Right after he throws, jump up as high as you can and nail him in the head with your axes. Bye-bye boss!

Ice Room Strategy

When you are inside the ice room and being attacked by falling icicles, just keep running straight and the icicles will just miss you every time. Another trick is to position yourself close to where the icicles will fall, and then, as they begin to fall, back away.

Skating Techniques

While you're "tearin' it up" on your skateboard, many snails, octopuses, and fish will try to knock you off your board. A trick to avoiding these attacks is to *keep on jumping.* Jump from cloud to cloud as quickly as you can and don't get hit.

1000 Free Points

On world 1-4, keep going until you see a red flower. You can't pick it up—it is a warning to you that a coyote is about to attack you from behind. Shoot him twice while jumping up. A picture of a Nintendo controller will appear, which will give you 1,000 points.

KARNOV

Overall Rating = 3
Challenge = 3.5
Sound and Graphics = 2.5

Story

Karnov, the hero in this story, is a well-built man who must find the treasure that was stolen from the town of Babylon. It was stolen by the mean and cruel dragon, RYU. Karnov must fight through nine levels before he encounters the dragon. This game can be continued as many times as you want.

Main Characters

FISH MONSTER—He will jump up and down while shooting things at you.

LION KEEPER—This man walks along at incredibly slow speeds while holding back a fierce lion. If you kill the lion first, the man will be easy, but if you kill the keeper first, the lion will go mad.

TYRANNOSAURUS—This fierce dinosaur is ruthless, and if you don't kill him right away, he'll knock you toothless! He will spit flaming fireballs at you.

MEDUSA SNAKE WOMAN—50% woman, 50% snake, 100% death.

ROCK MAN—He can become a bit of a nuisance after a while. Rock men (there are two different kinds) just stand on a ledge and heave rock after rock at you.

STONE MAN—He will curl up to look like a stone— just part of the scenery. Once you get close to him, though, he will come alive and throw knives at you.

BATS—These little creatures are pretty annoying, especially when they attack in groups.

GOLDEN KNIGHT—This character will stand in one place for a while. If you don't destroy him within a few seconds, he will explode into a whole bunch of deadly flying objects.

Hints

Fish Monster Trick

All you have to do to defeat this enemy is to crouch down and fire away. Once he jumps up and over to the left, run under him to the right and crouch down and keep firing. After he has jumped once or twice, the Fish Monster will be dead meat.

Bird Tip

On the second level, when you are underground and two walls are closing in and birds are attacking you from the sky, do this: Run to the far right, next to the wall, and turn around so that you are facing left. When the birds start to come down, fire your weapon rapidly, and they will all be destroyed before they have a chance to get you.

Secret Level SELECT

Do the following sequence when you see the title screen: While pushing to the right on controller 1, press and hold the A, B, and SELECT buttons all at the same time. Then, on controller 2, press the A button one time fewer than the number of the level you would like to start on. For example, if you want to start on level 5, press A four times.

Defeat Stoneheads

Stoneheads are those annoying little suckers that are always perched on top of large pillars firing bullets at you. The trick with them is to stand for a minute and watch their shots pass. Wait for a shot to pass you and jump over it. Jump up and fire one shot at the Stonehead. He will fire a shot up and then one down. After the lower shot, jump up and fire a second shot at him. Repeat this procedure one more time, and when one Stonehead is defeated, step up to the place where it was standing and use this trick on the next two Stoneheads.

Sea Serpent Trick

Sea serpents can be difficult, but not if you know how to handle them. Just wait for one to pass you, or better yet, swim under and around them so that you are behind them. Then, from the back, shoot at the serpent's head.

Keep Your Ladder

On the seventh level, you will get to an area where there will be a whole bunch of mummies and a gold door at the far right corner of the screen. You cannot go through that door, but when you touch it, a mummy and a ledge will appear. Since you used your ladder to get up to the ledge, jump to the left and over the mummy and retrieve your ladder. If you don't do this, you will lose your ladder permanently. Reposition it to the left a little and go back up it and kill the mummy. The easiest way to defeat mummies is to use a clapper, if you have one. Once the mummies are gone, move to the left of the screen and you will drop down through a trap door into the rest of the level.

Defeat Rex

The evil tyrannosaurus rex is a mean one, and he is difficult to defeat unless you have triple fireballs. With triple fireballs, just keep jumping and shooting at his head. If you don't have triple fireballs, the next best weapon to use is the boomerang, for it only takes one hit with the boomerang to permanently put this guy to sleep.

KID ICARUS

Overall rating = 2.5

Challenge = 3

Sound and Graphics = 2

Story

The Evil Medusa and her army have stolen the three sacred treasures of Angel Land. Also, she has transformed most of the people into stone statues. You are carrying only a bow and arrow, and your mission —should you choose to accept it—is to kill the Medusa and save all of the people. Throughout your journey, you will meet many of Medusa's guardians. When you defeat them, you'll be given hearts that you can use to buy weapons and power.

Main Characters

SPECKNOSE—He is a large flying nose with large glasses on and a fake-looking mustache.

MICK—He is just a large set of teeth that flies around and tries to bite you.

EGGPLANT WIZARD—This character will chase you and, if he catches you, will turn your body into an eggplant. If you have been changed into an eggplant, you must find a hospital to get some help.

KERON—This is a frog that can fly. He bites too, so be careful.

HEWDRAW—This is one of the bosses in the game. He is a large centipede-like snake.

REAPER and TWINBELLOWS—Two more enemies, along with: Monoeye, Mcgoo, Nettler, Kobil, Minos, Girin, Snowman, Reapette, Rokman, Keron, and Tamambo. Wow!

Hints

Treasure Room Code

If you break seven pots in a row without the Reaper appearing, the eighth pot will hold a valuable item. Break only the pots numbered 1, 2, and 8 in the black room and pots 2, 6, and 7 in the blue room shown in the maps. Break the pots in the order just given for best results. Then use the chart to help break all the other pots except for the one with the Reaper. Break the Reaper's pot last.

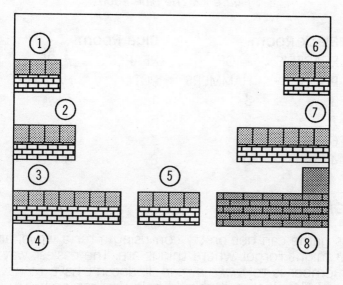

Figure K1. The Black Room

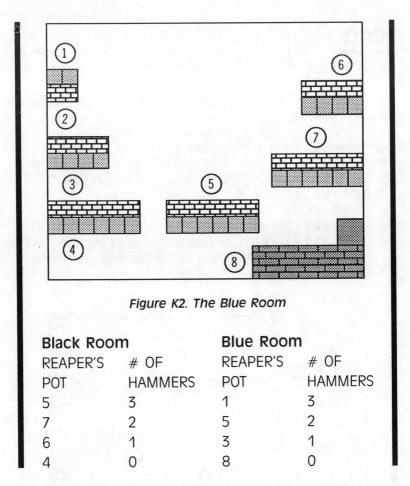

Figure K2. The Blue Room

Black Room		Blue Room	
REAPER'S POT	# OF HAMMERS	REAPER'S POT	# OF HAMMERS
5	3	1	3
7	2	5	2
6	1	3	1
4	0	8	0

Make Maps

This game can get pretty confusing after a while, and you might forget where things are. The easiest way to remember is to *make a map*. It doesn't have to have lots of details, but it should help you remember where important places like hospitals and shops are.

Use Money Wisely

During the game, you will encounter many shops. The men in the shops will sell different things, and they will almost always try to rip you off. Don't buy anything in the beginning except life potions or hammers, because you don't need anything (*and* you can't afford anything, either).

Store Bargaining

If you go into a store looking for a potion or something else, and the merchant is selling hammers and other items that you don't want, buy a hammer, since they only cost 20 hearts. After this purchase, a new merchant will come along, usually selling something different. If his prices seem too high, you can bargain with him by pressing both the A and B buttons at the same time.

Find the Hot Springs

When you find that you are getting a little low on energy, you will probably want to refill your supply at the Hot Springs room. To get from the starting point to the Hot Springs room in the fourth area of the realm of Twinbellows, you must go left twice, down through two rooms, and finally left through one room.

Defeat Hewdraw and Twinbellows

The trick to beating Hewdraw is to keep jumping up and over the centipede while aiming your shots at his head and face. The key to destroying Twinbellows is to hide behind one of the big pillars. That will protect you from his shots. When he gets near you, take a bunch of shots at him and jump over to the other side to hide in back of another pillar. Then repeat these moves.

Get the Credit Card

Using the trick described in the Treasure Room power tip, break all of the pots in a black room without the Reaper appearing. If pot 8 is the only one of the three pots (1, 2, or 8) that contains a hammer, then the Reaper is in pot 6. Break all the others, and finally pot 6 will reveal the Credit Card!

Find the Hospital

To find the Eggplant-healing hospital in the fourth area of the realm of Twinbellows you must go, from the starting point, three rooms to the right and one room up.

Medusa Tricks

For starters, you should know that you will not stand a chance of defeating this boss without the mirror shield, light arrow, and Pegasus's wings. When you get to her, go to the upper-left part of the screen, about ⅓ of the way from the right so that Medusa's shots will not hit you. When Medusa comes close, blast her in the eye, and follow her down to get in another shot. Keep following her until she dies.

LIFE FORCE

Overall Rating = 2.5

Challenge = 3

Sound and Graphics = 2

Story

Your goal in Life Force is to save the universe. During your mission you must avoid volcanic items, rapidly growing cells, spit balls, fire spheres, and crystal balls. You must fly through six stages: cell stage I, the volcanic stage, prominence stage, cell stage II, the palace stage, and finally the mechanical stage. Throughout the game, you must watch out for such enemies as Golem, Giga, the Tablus, and the Zakrons. Along the way, you collect 1-UPs and 5,000-point bonuses. In the end, you must defeat the Dragon and go on to destroy the Heart and Soul of Zelos to win.

Main Characters

GOLEM—He is a big brain that has only one weakness —his eye. He was appointed mayor of the first cell stage because all the aliens thought that brains were everything needed to run cells.

INTRUDER—You have to defeat him in the final battle of the volcanic stage. He somewhat resembles a robotic octopus. He's another one whose weak spot is his big blue eyeball.

CRUISER TETRON—The guardian of the prominence stage, Tetron is a huge dragon head that spits clouds of fire at you and your starship.

GIGA—He is a large, gross-looking skull that will spit bullets from his mouth and will release his eyes from their sockets to attack you. His weak spot is his open mouth.

TUTANKHAMANATTACK—Tut is protected by a ring of balls that circle around his head. He is difficult to beat, but you can do it.

THE HEART AND SOUL OF ZELOS—Zelos likes to eat planets and stars for a daily snack, and you must put an end to him. His dragon guards eat people in spaceships—like you!

TABLUS—They are enemies with no brains. The Tablus form lines when they attack to make it easy to defeat them.

GREMLINS—They come out of hatches on the sides of the walls.

Hints

120 Extra Men!

To start off the game with 30 free men, press UP, UP, DOWN, DOWN, LEFT, RIGHT, LEFT, RIGHT, B, A, START. You can do this three more times, each giving you 30 MORE men, totaling 120!

Defeat the Tabuls

When the Tablus come at you in a line, just position your ship on their level and shoot away.

Wait Up!

If you get to an area with rapidly growing cells, just stop your ship and take a break until the cells stop growing. It is dangerous to venture on while they are growing.

Defeat Golem

Since Golem's only weakness is his bulging eyeball, here is a strategy that should help you. Fly in circles round and round this monster, each time taking a few shots at his hideous eyeball. Sooner or later, he will explode into a cloud of smoke.

Hidden 1-UP

Just before you come up against the final enemy of the volcanic stage, you can blast the wall to the right of the passage to find a hidden 1-UP.

Fire Waves Trick

Right before the fiery tide comes in and turns you into toast, you will have a second's wait to prepare yourself. As soon as you spot one of these fire waves, maneuver your starship either up and over the wave, or under and through the middle.

Secret Bonuses and 1-UP

These locations are for the prominence stage only. The 5,000-point bonuses are located near the second flame, just after the ninth flame and close to the tenth flame. The only 1-UP in this stage is located just to the right of the fifth fire wave.

Defeat the Cruiser Tetron

The weak spot on the Cruiser Tetron is his head. Unfortunately, it spits fire at you. The technique we use is to fly around him and shoot at his head while also using the options. After a little work by you, the Cruiser Tetron won't be cruising any more.

Weapons Galore

At the beginning of the second cell stage, it's a good idea to position yourself toward the bottom of the screen and smack dab in the middle because this will enable you to get the most weapons.

Defeat the Giga

The Giga, like most living things besides bats, is completely blind without its eyes, so you should try to knock out his eyes first. Do this by spreading apart the Options so that you have wide firepower and then aim for the eyes. Now that Giga has no eyes, he won't know where to shoot!

Zakron Tip

When fighting the Zakron, make sure that you defeat him before you get too close to him, because all of the cells nested inside of him will escape and probably kill you.

Rib Bone Strategy

When facing the attack of the Rib Bone, just position yourself at the bottom of the screen and dodge its laser fire.

Attack Tutankhamanattack

This Tut has an indestructible force field of balls circling his face that can get quite annoying at times. The trick is to aim your laser beams at Tut's eyes when he changes colors.

Icicle Dodging

There is a safe spot on the screen when icicles fall during the palace stage. It is in the lower-right corner. Position yourself there quickly and none of the icicles will come even close.

Energy Dome

Just a little way into the palace stage is a small bump in the ceiling that appears to be part of the scenery. If you fly by it in the middle of the screen, you will be blasted off the planet. Get up to the top of the screen and back as far left as possible and open fire until the bump is destroyed, leaving an energy dome.

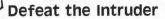

Defeat the Intruder

Like the style in which you defeated most of the other enemies, you must again aim for the Intruder's eyes. Move down to the bottom of the screen and knock out the three red capsules guarding the eye and then blow the sucker up!

Cease Fire!

When you get to the volcanic stage, you'll be attacked from all sides by Gremlins. Hatches will be on one side of the wall. If you go directly to the hatches and blow them up, you will be free of the Gremlin attacks.

Don't Waste Lasers

If you see a floating asteroid, you will probably want to shoot it. But if you do, you will be attacked by many shooting asteroid bits, and you will probably get hit. So save your lasers for your enemies.

Space-Age Mouthwash

Wash the aliens' mouths out with some spearmint lasers. Wait for the green faces in the mechanical stage to open their mouths and then *blast!*

MARBLE MADNESS

Overall rating = 2.5

Challenge = 2.5

Sound and Graphics = 2.5

Story

There's not much of a story to this game—no radioactive marbles, or marble princess to save—just you and your marble. You must roll your way through five stages of races and then on to the final race. Throughout the game, you will encounter hammers, catapults, vacuums, and lots of other obstacles, including slimes and marble eaters. Let's roll, baby!

Main Characters

BLACK BALL—This enemy will steal some of your time if you collide with it, but it can be easily dodged.

MARBLE EATER—This monster will temporarily stun you if you hit it, and if you stay in the same place for too long, this creature might eat you up!

SLIMES—If your marble even nicks the side of one of these acid-filled creatures, you will be dissolved into marble soup.

BIRDS—You will encounter these birds on the fifty level. They like to travel in groups, so you won't see just one or two. They move in a pattern, though, so you can easily dodge them.

Hints

Speed Is the Ticket

If you come to a point in the game that looks fairly easy or where there are no obstacles, hold down the A button for superspeed. This will let you finish the level faster.

Avoid Slimes

On stage 3, the intermediate race, you will get to an open area right after a narrow passage. You will see two raised platforms and a whole gang of slimes. If you get on the platform, none of the slimes will hurt you. So watch for an opening and roll!

Quick Escape

On stage 3, there is a place right in the beginning where you will see loads of Marble Eaters. It is right after the first steep downhill slope, where you see three diamond-shaped platforms. Quickly go along the right side of the cliff and roll away fast.

Moving Carpet

When you encounter the moving carpet on stage 3, stop and wait a while. Watch the carpet and the pattern it follows and then make your move.

Recycle Time

Once you become a pro at this game, you can risk moving at top speed throughout the whole level. This will get you time bonuses at the end, giving you more time for the next levels, which is very important.

Dropoff Dizziness

After a dropoff, you will feel dizzy for a second, and your marble will not move. After you regain your senses, be very careful not to go full speed off the edge of a cliff.

Which Path?

On stage 4, you will be catapulted up to a point where you have a choice of two paths. If you are a first-time player, we recommend the course to the left because it has wider paths and is safer. The path to the right is dangerous and has narrow paths, so be careful.

Bowl Over Hammers

Hammers appear out of nowhere just to ruin your day (or game). They will try to knock you right off the track, but all you have to do is go full speed ahead and ram right into them and run them over. Don't be afraid, just ram ahead.

Avoid Vacuums

Your first instinct when you see the large vacuums will be to panic. They'll try to suck you in, but you just have to build up a little speed and roll right by these suckers.

Dodge Walls

When you are in a situation where you must go through a very narrow passage, use your maneuvering skills to go straight through without touching the walls. If you hit the walls, you'll lose time.

Bonus Zone

During the Silly Race, you'll enter a bonus zone where the object is to smash your enemies. For each enemy squashed, you receive 3 bonus seconds to add to your time. So stay here as long as possible and smash *every* enemy so that you'll have extra time for the final race.

Save Your Time

To have success in stage 5, the Silly Race, it is best to have saved at least 40 seconds from stage three. To have any chance at all in the final race, you will need to have saved at least 50 seconds.

Birds

Birds are very tricky little characters and they move fast. They can be fairly destructive to your marble if they hit you, too. Make sure you stop and study their timing before trying to pass them.

MEGA MAN

Overall Rating = 3

Challenge = 3

Sound and Graphics = 3

Story

This story takes place in the future, in a city called Monsteropolis. Dr. Wright and Dr. Wily designed Mega Man, a superhuman robot that will serve the world and do some good. Unfortunately, Dr. Wily made six others and reprogrammed them to help him take over the world. Mega Man was not reprogrammed, and he is on a mission with Dr. Wright to stop Dr. Wily and his robots. Along the way, Mega Man must travel through six areas, each controlled by one of the reprogrammed robots. The seventh area is where Dr. Wily is hiding, and you must get there and defeat him to win the game.

Main Characters

CUTMAN—This robot throws large knives and swords at you. He is one of the six original reprogrammed robots.

GUTSMAN—You will smell the strongest and worst garlic breath you will ever smell as he smashes objects with his breath.

BOMBMAN—Another of the area leaders, Bombman throws bombs at you while furiously jumping up and down.

FIREMAN—He throws flaming fireballs at you, and boy is he ugly!

ELECMAN—This monster will really shock you with the bolts of electricity he spits at you.

ICEMAN—He fires large chunks of ice at you, and if you get too close, he'll give you his *cold stare*.

DR. WILY—He will be riding on a fully equipped flying saucer and will fire whatever he can to destroy you.

PICKET MAN—He will throw pickets at you while he protects himself with a shield.

Minor Characters

These are small enemies that you will encounter during your journey.

PENGS	OCTOPUSES
FLEAS	BEAKS
BLADERS	SHELLS, KILLER BULLETS
BOMBOMBS	WATCHERS
SCREW BOMBERS	BIG EYES

Hints

Defeat Iceman

Iceman will come at you with chunks of ice. He will throw three in a row and then take a short break. The trick here is to jump just after the first ice block arrives, but before the second one. In this way, none of the chunks of ice will hit you. Keep shooting through it all, though.

Picket Man Strategies

Picket Man will throw pickets at you. The easiest way to get a hit on him is to shoot him once and then back off for a little while. Wait until he fires a picket at you and then attack again with *just one* bullet. Keep doing this until he drops his shield, then blow him away!

Footholder Help

Jumping from footholder to footholder can be hard. Sometimes in your haste to get past that particular section with footholders, you will be shot by the footholder that you just left. To make sure you don't get fried, wait on the second footholder for the third one to pass once and hop on it after it comes back for a second time.

10X Bullet Power

Here is a little trick that will make one of your bullet shots count as a whole bunch of hits on a monster. Take your shot at the monster, and just as your bullet hits the enemy, start rapidly pressing the START button. Each time you pause and unpause the action, it will count as one hit on the monster. Try this trick on the rock monster in the Dr. Wily stage.

Stock Up on Power

You will often be in an area where you see an energy booster or two on the screen. After you get the energy, no energy will be left. But if you go out a door and then come back in, the energy booster will appear again. So, to stock up on energy, just find a door close to an energy booster and go in and out for a while.

Defeat Cutman

The trick to beating Cutman is to position yourself at the lower-right corner of the screen. He will jump up and down and when he jumps up and to the left, you should run under him to the right, quickly turn around and fire away. Before trying this, make sure you have a full energy tank. If you do, you can just stand in one place and shoot at Cutman, and you can be sure that he dies before you.

Disappearing Steps Pit

To get out of the first pit in Iceman's palace you must do the following: push up, up-left then jump down-right, then up-right followed by a move to the left. Next move up-right, jump up-left, and finally move to the left to exit.

Order of Operations

After Mega Man defeats an enemy, he gains that bad guy's powers. As a result, we have figured out the best order for you to follow. First, go after Cutman and use the blade on Elecman. Iceman should be next on your list because he is no match for the Elecman beam. Then go after Fireman because water (ice) never fails to put out his nasty fires. Then, when you spray fire on a bomb, it'll blow up, and that's exactly how you should defeat Bombman. Next, use your bombs on the last robot—Gutsman.

Don't Waste Time

Don't be a trigger-happy hunter, spraying bullets all over the screen at whatever you see. Save them! Even though there is no limit to your bullets or time, the more you screw around with your enemies, the more energy you are likely to lose. Don't waste your time on closed shells or pods, because you can't hurt them.

Flame Wall Truck

When you are in the Fireman empire, use your ice beam on the three walls made of hot flames. Position yourself at the bottom of the first pillar and shoot the first and second flames when they are at their lowest point. They will freeze in midair and you'll be able to jump up on them, freeze the third, and walk away.

Dodge Bombombs

In the Bombman empire, you will be constantly attacked by Bombombs. The way to escape from these attacks is to move along the platform you're on to the bottom of the tower. If you crouch low, none of the Bombombs will touch you.

Defeat Elecman

The trick to beating Elecman is to position yourself on the highest level of the screen and wait for him to shoot his electrical bolt. Then use your blades to finish this shocking villain off.

METAL GEAR

Overall Rating = 3

Challenge = 4

Sound and Graphics = 2

Story

You are on a mission to seek and destroy the secret weapon called Metal Gear. It is owned by the sinister Vermon CaTaffy. Your code name is Solid Snake, and you are equipped with a shortwave radio, some food, a handgun, a cardboard box, and a pack of cigarettes. (You probably won't use the cigarettes, but you'll use everything else.) Throughout the game, you can collect a possible 25 items of equipment and 8 different weapons, including missiles and a rocket launcher. You must travel through the desert, through four buildings, through maze zones, and fight men, tanks, and even dogs while you try to get into the main base. You must also collect eight access cards to get into certain doors.

Main Characters

SOLID SNAKE—This is your character. You must find the secret and unknown Metal Gear weapon and destroy it.

AGENT GREY FOX—One of your colleagues who has been captured by Vermon CaTaffy and is being held by the Outer Heaven group.

OUTER HEAVEN—This is the name of the group that is led by Vermon CaTaffy. They have designed the secret weapon Metal Gear.

COLONEL VERMON CATAFFY—The evil leader of the Outer Heaven group. He is a crazed lunatic.

SHOT GUNNER—He sprays bullets and he is the man that you have to take on. But first, you'll have to get out of the cell they put you in after they stole all of your weapons.

MACHINE GUN KID—He will also fire a spray of bullets at you, only faster than the shot gunner. He will follow you wherever you go.

BULL TANK—This mega tank will try to run you over, but if you use your grenade launcher, it can be stopped.

FIRE TROOPER—He'll shoot a long line of fire at you, and if you try to shoot him, his fire will destroy your weapon shots.

Hints

Fake Petrovitch

Inside building 2, specifically on floor 2, you'll find a tied-up prisoner. He will tell you that he is the Dr. Petrovitch you are looking for. Don't believe him, because if you try to rescue him, a large pitfall will open up and swallow you whole!

Be Patient!

You must be very patient in this game to succeed. When you start off in the jungle, a good trick is to wait for the enemies either to turn away from you or to fall asleep before you move on. Practice waiting at the top of each screen so that you don't get attacked by the enemies on the screen. This way you can avoid a fight.

Use the Maps

The detailed maps in the pack are useful. To find out where you are and where you want to go, pause the game and study the map. Make sure you don't walk up to a guarded door without the right card in your hand. Get the card out and ready *before* you approach the door. Also, use the maps to find out where the prisoners and secret weapons are located.

Secret Maze Exits

There are two different maze zones in this game, and we're going to tell you how to get out of both. When you get to the maze that leads you to the fourth building, you must take the left exit twice, then the left of the two upper paths, and finally the left exit again. For the maze that leads to building 5, go twice through the lower-left exit, once up, and finally take the lower-left exit.

Be Ready

You must be on your toes throughout the whole game, but especially when you are on your way out of a truck. When the screen comes up after you exit a truck, you will almost always be attacked by two, three, or even four armed soldiers. Be careful!

Save Prisoners

Look on the map, locate all of the nearby prisoners, and be sure to save them. Don't leave any, because for every five prisoners you save, your rank will increase by one star. You need to have a high rank to get certain things, like the compass and rocket launcher.

Ending Pass Code

To start your game of Metal Gear at the end right after the Super Computer has been destroyed, use this code and then go to the right a few screens: *WZRJZ QZZZD UJ51O UIQZZ NZRZE.*

Defeat Shot Gunner

Look on the map to find out where the shot gunner is located, and when you get to his screen, quickly run—without stopping—to the door on the bottom-right to get your equipment. Once you have all your weapons, you can hide behind the crates and bomb the shot gunner with your rocket launcher.

Fire Trooper Trick

The trick to defeating the Fire Trooper is to position yourself against the top right wall and, using your machine gun, fire an angled shot at him while you stay protected from his fire shots.

Rocket Launcher and Compass Secret

When we finally made it to the place to get the compass, and it was not there, we thought there was a malfunction in the game. The same thing happened with the rocket launcher! Now, after a year of moaning and groaning, we discovered that you must use your radio to contact Jennifer, code name *YO J YO J.* Once you talk to her on the radio, you can go into these rooms and get the items, for they will be there now. Keep in mind that you must have a rank of 4 Stars.

Bull Tank Techniques

You can only stop this tank by using the grenade launcher—you have no choice. You must get five clean hits on it before it gets you. A trick is to have the grenade launcher selected before you get inside the room and then fire shot after shot. When the tank gets close to you, just press SELECT and then come back to the main screen to find the tank back in its original starting position.

Blast Machine Gun Kid

This guy is a sitting duck, kids. All you have to do is stand behind one of the three barriers and bomb him with your grenade launcher, just like the shot gunner.

Stop That Pitfall!

Wow! We've found a nifty trick to pull when you come across one of those annoying pitfalls: Press SELECT and the pitfall will stop expanding! You have to act fast, though, so that it doesn't get very big. When you come back to the main screen, it will look like there is no pitfall at all, but beware, for it is still as big as it was when you pushed SELECT, and you can still fall in even though you can't see it.

The Great Escape

After you get arrested inside the truck in building 1, you will be put into a cell next to that of the kidnapped agent, Grey Fox. You will have no weapons but your bare hands, so go ahead and punch a hole in the left wall. (Sure, you can do it!) You must be sure to do this because agent Grey Fox has some really important information to give you.

Heat Panel Help

All of the magazines tell you to run across the heat panels very quickly, but make sure you have a lot of rations. That seems like a waste of food and energy. Try our trick: Stand on the nonelectrified space on the screen and fire your remote control missile at the heat panel switch. It may take a few tries, but it's a heck of a lot better than using up your energy!

Mega Weapons Code

This code will give you just about everything that you could possibly hold in your inventory: *5XZ1C GZZZG UOOOU UYRZZ NTOZ3.*

METROID

Overall Rating = 3

Challenge = 3

Sound and Graphics = 3

Story

You play the role of Samus Aran, the best outerspace hunter in the galaxy. You must travel through the planet Zebes in search of the Mother Brain. The Mother Brain is trying to carry out a plan to make lots of disgusting space creatures, called Metroids, to destroy the universe. Along the way, you must defeat two of the Mother Brain's gangsters: Ridley and Kraid. You have no time limit, but instead you have an energy meter. You may carry a maximum of six energy tanks, each holding 100 points of energy. You may also collect up to 255 missiles. Once you defeat the Mother Brain you must make an almost never-ending climb to get out of the planet Zebes. At the top of the climb, you will be royally shocked by the ending—guaranteed!

Main Characters

SAMUS ARAN—The space hunter sent out to defeat the Metroid breeding Mother-Brain, who is trying to destroy the universe.

RIDLEY—One of the Mother Brain's evil helpers in her plot to destroy the universe. He throws balls of fire at you.

KRAID—The very tricky and powerful boss found in the heart of Brinstar. He fires missiles at you.

Minor Characters

These are the enemies that you will encounter during your adventures. They hop, slide, crawl, jump, fly, and —if you're lucky—*die.*

ZOOMERS

ZELAS

ZEBS

SKREES

SIDE HOPPERS

RIOS

RIPPER

RIPPER II

NOVAE

MELLOWS

MULTIVIOLAS

VIOLAS

HOLTZES

DRAGONS

DESSGEEGAS

WAVERS

GEEGAS

MEMUS

Hints

Ouch! Lava!

If you accidentally fall into the burning lava, energy points will be deducted rapidly. The best thing to do in this situation is to *keep jumping.* Try to get back on a platform, but if you are nowhere near a platform, try to spend more time in the air than in the lava.

Get Maru Mari and Long Beam

The maru mari is located just to the left of the starting point of the game. Now that you can turn into a ball, get the long beam. Go right until you go out the door and into a passageway that only goes up and down. Go all the way up to the top and enter the door on the left. Once inside this door, travel left until you see the long beam.

Defeat Ridley

There are many keen ways to defeat Ridley. The easiest way is to stand as close to him as you can without stepping up to his level. His fireballs will not get you, and you can shoot away with your missiles. You can also try getting him from below. The third way —and the most fun—is to stand right under the blue door, shoot it so that it opens, and just before it closes, jump up and get stuck in the closed door. This will give you protection from his fire and you can still shoot your missiles at Ridley.

Escape Metroids

When you get to the end, you will be attacked by big blobs known as metroids. They will grab you and suck the energy out of you before you can say 1-2-3. The best way to defeat these suckers is to freeze them first, and then zap 'em with five missiles. They will reward you with either a lot of missiles or energy. If you fail, and they attack you, just curl up into a ball and try to madly bomb yourself out of there.

Get High Jump

The high jump can be found in Norfair. Find the purple vertical passageway and, moving down from the top, enter the sixth door you see. Head left until you find the missile door. There you go!

Jump High Without High Jump

Wow! All you have to do is turn into a ball and throw a bomb. Quickly press A to make yourself big again, and once you have been blasted into the air from your bomb, press the jump button. You'll be sent flying way up in the air, just as if you had done the high jump.

Shortcut to Tourian

This is more of a how-to trick. You will only be admitted into the final stage of the game after you have defeated Ridley and Kraid. Go to the top level of Brinstar and look for the room with the statues of Ridley and Kraid at the far left end of the large tunnel. Using your missiles, fire at the two statues. The statues will rise up and some blocks will complete the passageway across to the blue door. Roll across this passageway and you are in Tourian.

Bomb the Floors

When you are traveling through Norfair, you can be almost positive that every single floor can be bombed to reveal a secret passage. This is also true with a lot of the ceilings in Norfair. But be careful, for sometimes when you bomb the floor, you will fall into a trap!

Mother Brain Tips

When making your way past the Zee-betites to the Mother Brain, a trick is to freeze three Rinkas. Since only three Rinkas are allowed on the screen at once, no others can attack you. Next, when shooting the Zee-betites, stand on the ledge under them and jump up using *screw attack* while shooting missiles at them. Keep doing this until all five are destroyed. When battling the Brain herself, use the same technique of jumping up in a screw attack and firing when you get high

91

enough, do not stand on the bar because you will be knocked into the lava and probably never get out.

Order of Weapons

Here is the order we suggest you follow. First, get the maru mari and the long beam. Next go for bombs, followed by ice beam and varia. Then go on to get the screw attack and the high jump. If you want, you can get the wave beam, but we personally prefer the ice beam. Along the way, you must try to find all of the missiles and energy tanks. Hint: Leave one energy tank (the one hidden in the ceiling close to the beginning) for the end when you have to fight the Mother Brain.

Take Your Time

After you defeat the Mother Brain (*if* you beat her, that is), you'll have to jump from small platform to platform, up and up, to the end of the game. What will probably happen is you will be nervous that you won't make it in time and try to rush up the platforms. You will fall often and get very discouraged. Just take your time. You have almost enough time to have a Coke between steps. Just concentrate and remember to breathe.

Super Inventory

To start off your game with almost every possible weapon, use this code: *mMuiS1 II6-GE J1s?hO mOOWRM*. Wow! You are now a character that has a lot less armor on, revealing the true identity of Samus Aran. Another code that will give you a pretty

hefty load of equipment is *022400 A00000 G5?00e 0000cR.* If you do not want to bother with this code, try this one:
JUSTIN BAILEY ------ ------.

MICKEY MOUSECAPADE

Overall Rating = 2.5

Challenge = 2

Sound and Graphics = 3

Story

The two stars of this game are our old friends, Mickey and Minnie Mouse. They must travel in search of their missing buddy through five zones: the fun house, the ocean, the woods, a pirate ship, and finally a large castle. Remember that Mickey and Minnie are mice, so they must stay away from the fierce cats, jellyfish, lobsters, bears, and wasps. The only weapon that these poor mice can use is a throwing star, although they have to find their stars in treasure chests in the fun house. The fun thing about this game is that many of Walt Disney's movie characters are used. For example, once you are through the woods and into a magical garden, you'll meet up with the caterpillar from *Alice in Wonderland,* and the last battle of the game takes place in the castle of the wicked queen from *Snow White and the Seven Dwarfs.*

Main Characters

MICKEY MOUSE—The well-known Disney character has done it again. Aside from his movies, cartoons, amusement parks, T-shirts, underwear (a personal favorite!), and sleeping bags, he now has his own (well, shared) NINTENDO video game! He is only armed with throwing stars.

MINNIE MOUSE—She is also only armed with stars, although if you decide to warp, she will be left unarmed.

THE WIZARD—He is the bad guy in the fun house.

THE GATOR—This feisty alligator is the bad guy in the ocean.

PEGLEG PETE—One of this pirate's legs is a wooden peg, and he throws knives at you from every direction.

YELLOW PIGS—These annoying little porkies are always trying to sneak up on you from behind.

GUARDIAN ANGEL—The angel of invincibility will protect you for about 30 seconds if you find her.

BEARS—These large animals usually travel in pairs, so be careful! Some bears even throw honeycombs.

CATERPILLAR—Located in the garden just outside of the Winter Woods, the Caterpillar breathes rings of smoke at you.

THE EVIL QUEEN—She is hidden in the castle and is holding your lost friend as a prisoner.

Hints

Secret Continue

When your game has ended, and you see the title screen, quickly press and hold UP on the controller and then press START. You will continue from the beginning of the stage you died on.

The Order of Stars

At the start of the game, Mickey and Minnie have no weapons, and they must find their throwing stars. When you find the stars, be sure to get Mickey's stars before Minnie's.

Shoot Brooms

When you are attacked by the walking brooms, you must shoot at their handles, not their bristles. The easiest way to do this is to jump up and shoot at the same time.

Hidden Items

There is a way to tell if there is a secret item on the screen or near you. Shoot some of your stars into windows, trees, walls, barrels, or whatever is around. If a secret item is there, your star will hit it and make a puff of smoke. This is your signal to keep shooting (about seven or eight times) until that item appears.

Defeat the Wizard

Before you even attempt to battle the Wizard, make sure that you are at full strength. Climb up the ladder to the Wizard and start crazily jumping and shooting. After a whole mess of hits, the Wizard will blow up and disappear into thin air.

Don't Stop!

When traveling in the ocean area, make sure that you don't stand still for too long, or the mega wave will come out of the water and knock you into the sea.

Get Minnie's Stars

Exit the room that you got Mickey's stars from and go up three green rooms in a row. Next journey right through one blue room and two brown rooms. Finally go down two ladders in a row and to the left through a blue room. Wowee! We struck stars!

Play Straight

In Mickey Mousecapade, you can warp, but the smart move is to play all the levels in straight order. If you warp, only Mickey will be able to fire stars, and Minnie will be left unarmed.

Defeat the Crocodile

The ugly crocodile will try to swallow you whole unless you get to him first. Use the same trick you used to defeat the Wizard: Jump and shoot wildly until he is dead.

Correct Exits

When you are journeying in the spring or summer, the trick to finding the right exit is to go out of the second door you find. In the fall and winter, you must exit through a door hidden in one of the trees. In the fall, you'll find the hidden door right after you defeat the two bears. There will be a hole in the ground, and if you jump and throw your stars at the third tree to the right of this hole, the door will appear. To exit the winter and enter the final stage, continue in winter until you loop back to the Start sign. Jump up and fire some stars at the first tree to the right of the Start sign. It's a door!

Secret Items

In the pirate ship, you'll encounter some pretty savage enemies, and lose a lot of energy fast. A tip is to check everything, including barrels, for hidden items that might increase your strength.

Avoid the Pigs

Don't mess with the pigs, 'cause they ain't nothin' but porky troublemakers who will try to sneak up on you from behind. The easiest thing to do is just to jump over them and let them run off a nearby cliff.

Slow Scroll

When you are traveling in either fall and winter, it's a good idea to walk slowly, making the screen scroll slowly. This is useful for defeating bears one at a time when they try to come in pairs.

One at a Time

Some places you'll find it difficult to get both Mickey and Minnie to jump at the same time to the same place. When this happens, leave one of the mice behind and let the other do the work for a while.

Don't Stop—Again!

When you get to the garden right after the Winter Woods, make sure you keep moving and jumping, and keep your eyes peeled for holes opening in the ground.

 Hidden Energy

Always try to exit each level with full energy. In the garden, watch for small brown plants that fire missiles at you. Shoot six or seven missiles to get a diamond, which will bring up your strength to its max. In the castle and fun house, pieces of cake will give your energy level a boost.

MILON'S SECRET CASTLE

Overall Rating = 3.5

Challenge = 4

Sound and Graphics = 3

Story

Milon is on a mission to rescue the Queen of Hudson. The only form of communication in Hudson is the blowing of small flutelike instruments. A terrible man who hates music has terrorized Hudson and stolen the peoples' flutes and kidnapped their queen, Eliza. So the people now have no way to talk to each other and no ruler. Milon must travel through a magical castle where he must find his way through maze after maze looking for things that the queen has hidden. You must gather all of these items in order to pass all of the levels and defeat all seven demons in the game.

Main Characters

MILON—He is the only person in the whole town of Hudson who cannot tell the difference between two notes, so he can't understand the language. Still, he is on a mission to save the Queen of Hudson.

BEE—If you can catch this quick bee, you'll be rewarded with a shield to protect you.

NOTES, SHARPS, AND FLATS—These are the main characters in the bonus stages that you can access by catching a music box. If you catch a note or a sharp, you will be given bonus points. But if you catch a flat, you'll lose points.

FLAME MEN—These hot monsters will spit fire at you.

DEMONS—These are the enemies that await you at the end of each level. Be sure you have the proper items before entering the demon rooms.

OCTOPUS—When you destroy this eight-legged creature, he will turn into a balloon that will carry you up and out of the well.

Hints

Money X 3

Wow! Get three times the money you see in this room. It is on level 3, at the upper-left corner. Even though this room has a ton of money in it, once you get it all, you can exit and enter two more times! Wow!

Flame Men Tip

When you encounter the red-hot Flame Men, don't bother wasting your time shooting them, just dodge them. They are a pain to try to destroy and easy to get around.

Secret Store

When you get to the point where HUDSON is written in large letters at the bottom of the screen, shoot the N. After shooting through the N, a secret door to the shop that sells the fireproof jacket will appear.

Get Your Stuff

In order to fight the demon at the end of each stage, you must have collected all of the important items. If you don't have the right stuff, the demon will not be in the room when you come. For the first floor demon, make sure that you have the spring shoes and the shrink potion.

Secret Stuff

Here's a little tip that usually helps us succeed: In *every* room of the castle, make sure to shoot the blocks in the four corners of the room in order to check for hidden things. These hidden things might be money icons or secret doors to shops, or other interesting things.

Get the Spring Shoes

When you are in the first room of the castle, three blocks are on the ground level. Shoot the two outside blocks and push the middle block to the left. Fire at the spot where the block you just pushed used to be and a secret door will appear, leading you to the spring shoes.

Endless $$Money$$

A room on level 3 has a fireplace in the lower-right corner. This room also is the home of a lot of money. Shoot the blocks in the lower-left corner to reveal some money blocks. Exit the room and then come back in. You'll be able to shoot the blocks for more money.

Electric Ice

Be careful of the ice blocks that have an electric current running between them. If you stand right under the current, the hidden springs in the floor will propel you up into the air and through the electricity! You will probably die.

Secret Continue

This Continue function can only be operated if you have defeated the first-floor demon and picked up the crystal he left behind. Once you've done that, you can continue after you die by pressing LEFT and START at the same time.

Elevator Tip

Before you get on the elevator, you *must* have the feather. Otherwise you will be too heavy to ride on the elevator. Well, since you can't ride the elevator, you might as well do something else in that room. Try shooting the blocks in the upper-right area of the screen to reveal a hidden store and shooting the blocks in the lower-right corner on the wall to get a honeycomb.

Get the Saw

You need the saw to get the demon on the second floor. First, you must buy the vest for $25 and also buy the lantern. The first floor has a store with a real expensive ($50) lantern, but the second floor is having a Blue Light Special on $15 lanterns. Next, go into the well from floor 2, using the lantern for light and the vest for protection. Inside the well, you will get the hammer. Use the hammer while standing on the platform to the left of the entrance to the Shrink Potion room. A door will appear that leads you to the Saw.

Tower Maze Ending

When you get inside the tower, you'll be stuck in an endless maze. There is, of course, a secret exit. Shoot the blocks in the upper-right corner of the screen to reveal the exit.

Mega Bubbles

When you are in the well, make sure that you do not climb out. Instead, catch the balloon for a joy ride. Later on, when you are battling the third demon, you will notice that your bubbles are bigger and stronger.

The "Right" Magician

On the fourth floor, you will find five magicians, four of which are imposters. The way to tell which magician to kill is to watch, and if he fires at you with an open cape, he is genuine. To kill him, dodge his bullets and shoot at him when his cape is wide open.

Fake Queens

There are two tower rooms with a room in between them. This middle room is the home of the fake queens. *Do not* go between the pillars or you'll be trapped by the trap doors. Try shooting into open space, because that will reveal invisible blocks.

Get the Scepter and Crown

To get the crown and scepter of Queen Eliza, you must go into the room of the fake queens and touch both queens, making two birds appear. Then you must defeat these birds to earn the scepter and crown. Beware, though, because you cannot do this unless you first gain possession of the canteen.

NINJA GAIDEN

Overall rating = 3

Challenge = 3

Sound and Graphics = 3

Story

Before Ryu's father was killed in a duel, he sent Ryu a telegram telling him to get the Dragon Sword and bring it to the U.S.A. Ryu is determined to get back at the murderer, but he must journey through 6 rounds and 20 areas. He must fight many enemies, including boxers, ninjas, wizards, cougars, and bats. Then he must defeat five bosses and, finally, a large monster at the end.

Main Characters

DOGMAN—Half dog, half man; you can only defeat this character if you are kneeling.

BARBARIAN—The "South American Executioner" is part of the Malice Four group. You must kill him in Jay's Bar.

The BOXER—You must stay low to defeat him. He is a tough little cookie.

BOMBERHEAD—This man has an iron fist, and he wears spikes all over his body. He is the Act 1, Area 3 guard.

THE EAGLE—When an Eagle swoops down on you, you lose three levels of Life.

BASAQUER—Jaquio forced him to join the Malice Four against Ryu. He used to be a member of the F.R.O.D. (Five Ranges of Doom), and he sprays bullets out in all directions to kill you.

KELBEROSS—He is the Guardian of Act 4, and he is *mean.* He hops around and shoots at you.

Hints

 Hidden Items

Act 1, Area 1: STREETLIGHTS (Same for Stage 2)

Act 2, Area 1: LIGHTS HANGING ON THE WALLS

Act 2, Area 2: HOVERING ANTS (Same for Stage 3)

Act 3, Area 1: BUTTERFLY

Act 3, Area 2: WHITE-HEADED EAGLES (Same for Stage 3)

Climb Between Walls

If you would like to climb up between two walls, you must press the A button to jump and then quickly press back and forth from left to right on the controller.

Avoid Enemies

On Act 1, Area 1, you will come to a point where there are three signs. Climb up to the top of the first sign and jump to the second and third signs. You will avoid a few enemies this way.

Defeat Barbarian

When the Barbarian attacks you, get down low and avoid his deadly axe. Use your sword on him while you are still crouching down, and he will be a piece of cake! Another way to defeat the Barbarian is to hit him with your sword, then climb up and hold onto the wall and wait for him to pass. Come back down and repeat these moves again and again.

Bomberhead Weaknesses

Bomberhead is the Act 2 boss, and he has a weakness. The best time to hit him is when he has his chain and sickle weapon in the air. If you need to get away from Bomberhead and take a rest, just climb up one of the walls.

Jump to the Top!

On 1-1, when you see two signs, one above the other, you can get to the top of them by doing five wall-spring jumps in a row.

 **Defeat Basaquer**

When fighting Basaquer, you must position yourself under the rock formation at the top and use your sword to block the bullets. When he jumps close to you, move in toward him and attack.

Hawk Attack

Be careful when you try to cross the small step-platforms in the water, for once you get down on the steps you will be attacked immediately by a fierce hawk. Jump up and shoot him in midair.

Yomi's Cave Tip

There will be a very rude man outside of Yomi's Cave. He will be firing a bazooka at you, and you must be very quick to dodge his shots and get around him— or even shoot him. Whatever you do, do it *fast.*

Defeat Kelbeross

A trick to defeating the Guardian of Act 4 is to stand to the left of him and wait until you have an open shot at him. Then throw your Windmill Throwing Star at him. He will usually disappear after one shot, but if not, keep throwin' those stars!

Bonus Windmill Star Use

When you get to the ice stages, at a certain point you will be given a free Windmill Star that you will need. As a matter of fact, be on your toes, because you will need it just a few seconds after you pick it up!

Extra Man

To get an extra man at the start of Act 4, you must defeat a spider. He will be jumping around near the bottom of the screen. To be sure it's the right spider, you must kill them all.

Hall of Demons Tip

When you get into the Hall of Demons, you will see two UGLY demons. Position yourself between them and wait for the demons to come down. When they do, use your sword on them. Better yet, use a fire-wheel.

Final Battle Musts

It is an *absolute must* to have at least 99 units of Spiritual strength if you want to have a chance at winning the final battle.

Watch Out!

You will be unpleasantly surprised when you are climbing up a cliff to a fallen tree branch. With no warning at all, the bird on your right will dive down and around and come up to attack you from the left side! If you don't act fast, you will be eaten alive by the bird.

Red Execution Boss Trick

When you encounter the boss at the Place of Red Execution, all you have to do is get up real close and hit him over and over again with your sword. Make sure that you don't touch him—only your sword can touch him.

SUPER MARIO BROS.

Overall Rating = 3.5
Challenge = 3
Sound and Graphics = 4

Story

The Mushroom Kingdom has been raided by the cruel King Bowser, and of course he picked up Princess Toadstool for a souvenir. Mario, the star of the show, must journey through 32 levels before he can finally have a shot at defeating King Bowser. However, Mario must dodge hundreds of Koopas that are under the rule of the king before completing his quest. Mario has the talent to become one of three forms: Small Mario, Super Mario, and Fiery Mario. This game has an endless number of quests, but only two different difficulty levels.

Main Characters

MARIO—The hero of the story starts small, but he can change into Super Mario and Fiery Mario.

LUIGI—He has the exact same abilities as Mario, but he has a different name and he is used for the second player.

HAMMER BROTHERS—These small versions of King Bowser jump up and down while throwing hammers at you.

BLOOPERS—These little creatures live under the water and somewhat resemble jellyfish.

BUZZY BEETLE—You can only defeat this little beetle by stomping on it because he is impervious to fireballs.

PIRHANA FLOWERS—These are man-eating Venus Flytraps that live in the pipes.

CHEEP-CHEEPS—These are commonly known by humans as fish. They can also fly if they are taken out of the water.

BULLET BILL—He is a large bullet that is shot from cannons that are very common on world 7.

SPINY—He is a spiked enemy that can only be destroyed by Mario or Luigi's fireballs.

GOOMBAS—These are the little green turtles that are extremely common in this game.

Hints

 Warp Zone Locations

There are three warp zones in this game, and the proper use of two of them will bring you to level 8 in no time at all.

The first warp zone is on level 1-2, and it will warp you to world 2, 3, or 4. Go to the end of the level, to the point where you are on an elevator right before a pipe that leads to the end of the level. Ride the elevator all the way to the top and jump off onto the row of bricks at the top of the screen. Run all the way to the right and warp!

The next two warp zones are on world 4-2. The warp to world 5 is at the end of 4-2. Use the technique you used for the warp on level 1-2. To warp to world 6, 7, or 8, go to the area in the beginning right after the first elevator. There will be three bricks close to the top left of the screen. Stand directly under the far right brick and jump up to reveal a hidden coin. Do the same for the brick to the left of it, and then (moving to the left) *skip a brick.* Skipping a brick reveals the hidden brick one space to the left of the skipped brick. Get up on the bricks that you revealed and bop the far left brick that is over the space that you skipped over. A beanstalk will appear, and when you climb up it, you will be in the warp zone. Refer to Figures M1, M2, and M3 for help.

Figure M1. First Warp Zone

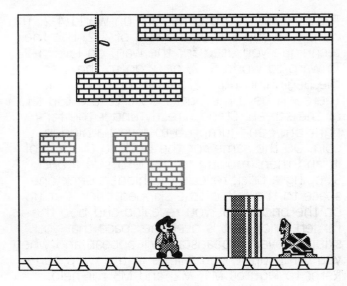

Figure M2. Second Warp Zone

Figure M3. Third Warp Zone

Hammer Brothers Trick

Here is the trick that has brought us enough success to win this game eight times in a row. Basically, you are going to want to "dance" with the Hammer Brothers. Get up real close to one of them, so that you are facing him. Don't touch him, but let his hammers fly over your head. You must be careful because they move back and forth. You can't stand in one place, you must move with him—*dance!*

Fireworks Secret

At the end of each level, you jump onto a flagpole and slide down it. If you hit the flagpole at a certain time, some fireworks will be set off in the sky. To determine how many fireworks you get, just look at the last number of the time you hit the flagpole. If it is a 1, 3, or a 6, you'll get that number of fireworks. The trick we use to get 6 fireworks is to wait until the last digit is 9 and then start running.

Secret Continue

Yes, like many games, there is a secret Continue feature built in to the game. If you use up all of your Marios, press the START and A buttons at the same time. You'll start with 3 Marios back at the beginning of the level where you died.

Water Safety

When you get to the water stages (2-2 and 7-2), here's a little trick to use to avoid getting hit by the Bloopers. As soon as you enter the level, madly press the A button over and over again while pushing to the right. You should go through most of the level at the top of the water. If you stay at the top, you won't get hit by any enemies until you reach the whirlpool.

World 7-4 Secret

The evil King Bowser did not want to make your journey easy, so he set a whole bunch of traps and mazes. Level 7-4 is a maze, and if you go through it in the wrong manner, it will seem endless. The secret to the maze is to go down, then middle, then up. There are three levels of platforms, and the way to get through the maze is to go on the ground floor until you see a break in the level above you. Hop up to the middle level and run until you see a break in the upper floor. Hop up, over the hole, and go to the right until you get to the second part of the maze. The trick here is exactly the same, so use it and go get the Mushroom Retainer (Fake Princess).

Endless Minus World

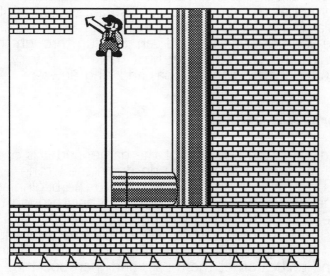

Figure M4. Endless Minus World

At the end of world 1-2 there is a secret entrance to the neverending water level, labeled world −1. To get in, go to the end of world 1-2 until you see the pipe that would usually bring you up and to the flagpole. Stand on the pipe and jump up to break the second and third bricks from the right. *Do not* break the brick that is touching the pipe, but instead, *do* get your head stuck in it. To do this, you must position yourself at the far left edge of the pipe and jump up into the air. When you are higher than the brick, push to the right so that your head gets stuck in from the left side of the brick. This is a very difficult trick, but once you do it, go to the right and go in one of the outside tubes to enter world −1.

Mario Sacrifice

If you find yourself in big trouble, you can do one of two things: You can either sacrifice Super Mario or you can ask a friend to help. If you are Super Mario and you get hit, you don't die. Instead, you shrink to regular Mario and become invincible for 5 seconds. While you are invincible you can just run through the enemies and you won't get hurt. This trick is very useful for battling the Koopas and King Bowser.

World 8-4 Secret

World 8-4 is the last level of the game, and it is one large maze for Mario. If you go down the wrong pipes, you will be warped way back to the beginning of the level and have to try again. To get through the maze, you must keep going until you see the third pipe in the whole level. Go down that pipe until you reach a floating pipe and two jumping turtles. Either kill the turtles or let them pass and then bop the invisible coin box that is located two blocks to the left of the pipe. Get on the block, jump onto the pipe, and go down it. Then go to the right and go down the third pipe that you see. Swim your way through the water world, but be patient and don't get hit! When you get out, don't go into the next pipe. Instead, find some way to get around the Hammer Brothers and jump up to the level that holds the mighty mean King Bowser. If you are Super Mario, you can try to get under him, but if you get hit, quickly touch the axe and you'll win the game.

100 Extra Men

This is a difficult trick to explain in text, but here goes. Go to the end of world 3-1, where two Koopas are walking down the stairs toward you. Quickly get against one of the bottom stairs and jump up when the Koopa is about two stairs above you. You want to land on the left edge of the Koopa when he is halfway off the stair. He will bounce once and stop. Make sure you *do not move* the controller, but press the A button to jump up on him. Keep jumping until you are jumping and bouncing on him automatically. This will give you many extra lives and make some nice bell music, too. Be careful, though, because if you get too many men, you will overload and the game will end.

SUPER MARIO BROS. 2

Overall Rating = 3.5
Challenge = 3
Sound and Graphics = 4

Story

One night while Mario was asleep, he had an incredible dream. He dreamed that he saw a tall, winding stairway and that he climbed to the top. At the top of the stairs was a large door, and Mario—being the adventurous character we know him to be—opened the door. He hopped right in and found that he was in some sort of fantasy land. He found out that he was summoned to save the land of Subcon from the mean toad, Wart. To do this, Mario and his three friends, Luigi, Princess Toadstool, and Toad, must adventure through 20 different levels of pure playing satisfaction. Good Luck!

Main Characters

MARIO—He can jump about the average height of the four people, but he jumps lower when he is carrying an item.

LUIGI—Luigi can jump the highest of them all, but if he is carrying something, he loses some of his ability, too.

TOAD—He jumps the lowest, but can pick up items the fastest, and he runs the fastest with something on his back.

PRINCESS—She has the ability to hover over the ground for about 1½ seconds. This is extremely useful in tricky situations.

BIRDO—This animal spits eggs and fireballs at you and appears many times throughout the game.

MOUSER—He throws bombs at you. You must catch them and throw them back to kill him.

TRYCLYDE—He has three heads and spits fireballs at you. It takes three hits to kill him.

FRYGUY—Once you kill this fiery monster, he breaks into six mini Fryguys. He is tricky!

WART—This oversized toad created all of these monsters by playing with his invention—the Dream Machine. He must be hit six times by vegetables to be killed.

Hints

Stopwatch

Remember to count the number of large vegetables that you pull out of the ground, for when you pull up the fifth veggie in a row, a stopwatch appears, which will freeze all of the characters for a while.

Mushroom

In world 1-2, immediately after flying across the sky on the magic carpet, there will be two jars. Right before the first jar is a magic potion. Pick it up, throw it between the two jars, go in the door, and you will get a mushroom.

Easy Extra Men

After completing each level, you have a chance to "play the slots." You can play for extra men, using as many coins as you collected on the past level. The second item that appears in the first box is *always a cherry!* If your timing is correct, you can soon master this trick and gain many extra men.

Kill Fryguy

The trick to beating Fryguy is to gather all of the mushrooms from the bottom of the screen and bring them up to the top. Once you are up there, pick up a mushroom and wait until Fryguy flies near you. Throw the mushroom at him so that it hits him and also lands back on the platform at the top. After he is dead, you will have ammo to use to kill his little friends.

Ditch Phanto

When you enter PHANTO's secret hideout, you must act fast. The second you grab the key, Phanto comes to life and flies after you. Throw the key immediately and Phanto will fly away. Pick it up and throw it again if you see Phanto return. After you do this two or three times, Phanto will give up.

Shortcut to World 7

At the beginning of world 6-1, you will go up a ladder. To your left is a wall with quicksand under it. Push left on the control pad until you are touching the wall. Allow your man to begin sinking into the quicksand until he is almost covered. All the while, keep pushing left and hitting the A button over and over until you have made it to the other side. Be careful—if you sink all the way over your head, you'll die. Go in the door and into the pyramid to the left.

Get Two POWs

This trick works anytime during the game. Throw a potion near a POW and go in the door. In Subcon, pick up the POW and wait for the time to run out. When you get outside, you'll be holding a POW, and a POW will be on the ground!

Extra Man

On world 1-2, when you get to the first jar, go down into it. You'll find a plant inside the jar. When you pick it up, you will find that it is a 1-UP mushroom. Yippee!

Secret Waterfall Island

At the beginning of world 3-1, when you see a door with a waterfall to the right of it and a cloud above it, slide down the waterfall (see Figure MM1). Carefully go to the center of the screen as you are sliding so that you land on the platform. Go in the door and you will find 15 plants. Pick up the 10th one (a potion) and throw it to get 14 coins (if you're fast enough!). But wait, there's also a warp zone! Go out the door and come back in, get the potion, and throw it at the far right next to the jar. Go in and warp to world 5.

Figure MM1. World 3-1

Kill Ostro

When you are fighting Ostro, watch the number of eggs he spits at you. After he spits three eggs in a row, he will pause to catch his breath. Now is a good time to throw one of his eggs back at him.

Defeat Tryclyde

You will find six mushroom blocks inside Tryclyde's lair. Pick them up one by one and quickly pile them up to form a protecting wall. This will block his fireballs, which you can take off the top and throw back at Tryclyde.

Secret Warp Zones

Jumping from one world to another is one of the most exciting ways to progress in Super Mario Bros. 2.

How to Kill Wart

For this trick, you are better off using Luigi, so choose him at the beginning of the level. On world 7-2, you will encounter Wart. We have found a special trick that works every time. Stand on the first platform and wait for a vegetable to pop out. Grab it while holding onto the B button and run quickly and jump all the way over Wart. You are now in the corner of the screen, and Wart cannot harm you. Jump up and throw your veggie at the toad when his mouth is open. Then jump back over Wart and repeat this process five more times. Go for it, because the ending is magnificent.

Warp to World 4

The way to warp from world 1-3 to world 4-1 (a small but helpful warp) is to go to the far right end of the last part of the level, past the final door, and pick up the potion. To warp to world 4 (see Figure MM2), enter the vase when you're in Subspace.

Figure MM2. Warping to World 4-1

Warp to World 5

You must slide down the waterfall on world 3-1. When you get inside the room with many plants, get the tenth plant, which is a potion, and throw it near the vase at the far right. Enter the vase in Subspace and warp to world 5 (see Figure MM3).

Figure MM3. Warping to World 5

Warp to World 6

This warp is on level 4-2 with icy walkways and whales. You will find a platform with a vase and nothing else on it. You can't go into the vase, so you must get a potion from somewhere before this on the level and throw it on that platform. In Subspace, go into the vase and you will warp to world 6 (see Figure MM4).

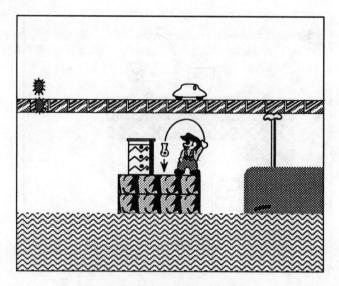

Figure MM4. Warping to World 6

Warp to World 7

Right after you go up the ladder in world 5-3, you will see a vase and two plants on the level above you (see Figure MM5). Make sure you are Luigi and do a squatting jump onto the level above you. Go to the left and get a potion and throw it near the vase. When in Subspace, enter the vase and you will warp to world 7 (see Figure MM5).

Figure MM5. In World 5-3

ULTIMA EXODUS

Overall Rating = 3

Challenge = 4

Sound and Graphics = 2

Story

This game is actually the third part of a series that
has been made for personal computer systems. In
the first two parts, a magician named Mondain and
a nasty witch called Minex were conquered and now
they want to get their revenge. They have joined
forces and are planning to conquer Britannia with

their evil clan called Exodus. Your job is to journey with three other men to the Island of Fire where Exodus is hiding out.

The interesting thing about this game is that you can be 1 of 55 different characters. You can choose from 11 occupations: Lark, Cleric, Wizard, Fighter, Barbarian, Paladin, Thief, Illusionist, Alchemist, Ranger, or Druid. Once you have picked an occupation, you can choose your character's race: Fuzzy, Dwarf, Elf, Bobbit, or even Human. Then you must travel through 10 cities and 7 dungeons and finally to the Heart Island of Fire to battle Exodus. The game will give you months and months of fun and excitement, just like the two Zeldas did.

Main Characters

These are the *races* of the characters that you can choose from.

HUMAN	DWARF	ELF	FUZZY	BOBBIT

These are all of the *occupations* of the characters that you can choose.

CLERIC	FIGHTER	THIEF	RANGER
LARK	BARBARIAN	ILLUSIONIST	DRUID
WIZARD	PALADIN	ALCHEMIST	

These are your enemies.

ZOMBIES	SNAKES	GOBLINS	PIRATES

. . . AND OTHER EVIL CREATURES

Hints

Run Away from a Fight

In many cases, running is the best thing to do. If you are near a house and you are confronted by a mean-looking enemy, duck into the house for a while. When you come out, he probably will have left. But in case he hasn't, just go back in the house for a bit and try again.

Build Up Experience

A smart thing to do is to hang around the beginning of the game for a while and just keep killing the lame and weak enemies with your Repel and Undead spells. These enemies, like Orcs, are very simple to kill and will give you experience points. You must have at least 600 experience points before you enter Lord British's castle because once you leave the castle, the enemies will be a lot stronger than before.

Selecting Characters

Here are some helpful hints for selecting your character. When choosing a character that is already made, try to find one who has a lot of wisdom points. This is important because buying wisdom during the game is not cheap. Don't select the Ranger or the Fighter because of their bulging muscles—choose a smart guy. Later you can buy strength for these muscle-bound characters. Or you can design your own character with the 50 points given to you. If you construct your own character, make sure that you get both the Repel and Undead spells.

Buy Wisdom

The reason you need to have a lot of wisdom is so you can perform more advanced and powerful spells. But, alas, wisdom is only for the rich—at 100 pieces of gold for each point of wisdom. The place to buy wisdom is in the Shrine of Intelligence. You must first get a whirlpool, though. Then try all of the different shrines to find the right one.

Keep Your Eyes Out

Every once in a while, check on the food level of each of your characters. If your food runs out, you'll lose a lot of hit points because the points are automatically taken off for every step you take without food. When you are even close to low on food, find a market and stock up.

Direct Hit!

When fighting Ghouls and Skeletons, always use the Undead spell. You will find that sometimes you will get a hit and other times you will get a miss. What you get depends on the enemy's position. If the Ghoul has his club up, it will be a hit. If the skeleton's arms are both out, it will also register a hit. If either enemy is in its other stance, it will be a miss.

Las Vegas a la Britannia

Britannia has gambling casinos, like Las Vegas. They play slightly different games, though. You can bet 10, 50, or 100 pieces of gold on the old "Stone-Scissors-Paper" game. It is probably the easiest way to make—or lose—a whole lot of money. Watch out, though, because Stone-Scissors-Paper is addictive!

Moon Phases

Take full advantage of the different moon phases. When the moon is in its crescent stage, the Moon Gates will open, allowing you to transport yourself to an unknown destination. You can only do this on a crescent moon, though, so keep your eye on the upper-left corner of the screen.

Secret Reincarnation

If one of your characters dies, and you want him back, do this: Go all the way back to the beginning point and *save your game.* Create a brand new group of four and let all of them die as fast as you can. Only three are allowed to die. Once three men are dead, save the game again. Then make a new party using the dead man from your first party as the leader and the three dead people as the rest of the group. The lead character will come back to life because you are not allowed to have more than three dead people. Then save the game one last time and rejoin the revived character with his original party.

Booby Traps

Be careful when opening chests that are laying on the ground, because not all of them are Treasure Chests. More times than not, they have booby traps inside them that will take off some Hit Points. In fact, just about every chest is booby trapped!

Entrance to the Castle

There are only two entrances to the evil castle where Exodus is hiding out. The easier one to use is near a dock that is guarded by a snake. Find this snake and defeat it in order to reach the entrance behind it. The only other entrance is through the moon gates, but that is a very tricky way to go.

Ride 'em Horsie!

Horses can prove to be an extremely worthy investment, for they can really move. They let you travel through Britannia a lot faster, even though they are pretty expensive. The good thing about them is that you can fit all four of your adventurers on one horse.

ZELDA II—THE ADVENTURE OF LINK

Overall rating = 3.5

Challenge = 4

Sound and Graphics = 3

Story

A mighty sorcerer cast a sleeping spell on Princess Zelda, and in order to save her, Link must find the third piece of the Triforce. He has the first two pieces—Power and Wisdom—and now he must get Courage. He must journey through Hyrule to the Great Palace. Good luck!

Main Characters

LINK—The hero of our story who is off to rescue his beloved Princess Zelda.

IRONKNUCKLE—One of the palace guardians, he wears full armor, rides a horse, and carries a lance.

HORSEHEAD—This peculiar character is just a large head of a horse!

BARBA—A nasty sea serpent that is another palace guardian.

HELMETHEAD—A man in full armor who carries a flaming sword.

CAROCK—He is some sort of monster who wears rags as clothing, a skull around his neck, and who casts spells over you. He is one tricky guy, so watch out!

Hints

Hot Clues

Whenever you meet somebody in a town, he will talk to you. The best clues, though, come from the people that have just stepped out of their houses.

Ironknuckle Magic

From the second palace, you can uncover a secret in all of the Ironknuckle statues. Hit the head (visor) of the statue and one of two things will appear. Either the statue will come to life (Uh-Oh!) or a Red Magic Potion will appear. Cool!

Kill Horsehead

Since Horsehead wears no helmet, he is easy to kill. Just jump into the air and strike him on the head with all your might.

Get the Glove

The Glove is hidden in Midoro, the swamp palace. From the entrance, take the elevator down one screen, go left four screens, down one, and left two more times to get the Glove.

Get the Fairy Spell

Find a cave that is north of Saria. It is guarded by a single rock that you must break to get in the cave. Inside the cave is the Sacred Water. Bring the Sacred Water to the woman in the town of Mido who has a sick daughter. If you give the Sacred Water to this woman, she will reward you with the Fairy spell.

Secret Teleport

Go to an area in one of the palaces where blocks fall from the sky. Let all the blocks fall down to form a solid wall. Climb up the wall and when you get to the top, use the Fairy spell. Press the A button to make Link turn into a fairy. Then press either left or right, and Link will be teleported to the roof of that palace. Once on the roof, activate the Fairy spell again and press either left or right. You'll be teleported to the ceiling of a palace that has the same floor and enemies as the first palace, but it will have the color and walls like the palace that you just left. This trick does not help your character, but it is fun to do.

Get the Candle

The candle is located in the first temple. It is not hard to find, so we won't ruin the fun, but you should know that you'll need it to go through some of the dark caves later in the game.

Special Present

To get your special present, you must go to the town of Rauru very early in the game. You'll not only receive a gift, but also some valuable information about your quest.

Ironknuckle Strategies

If an Ironknuckle attacks you near an elevator, get on the elevator and ride up a little bit so that when you strike him, your weapon hits his head. When he starts to get on the elevator, get off and hit him until he dies.

Statue Magic

On the steps of most of the temples, you will see a stone statue. Hit it with your sword, and a jar of potion will appear.

Get the Raft

The raft is hidden in the Island Palace. From the start, you must take the elevator down and go to the right until you have a chance to go down again. Immediately go right two screens and you will find the raft. Yippee!

Quick Experience

This trick only works if you have a character that has already won the game. Select this character and conquer the first palace. After you place the jewel in the statue, you will be given 9,000 experience points. Just as your points begin to rise, press PAUSE. On controller 2, press Up and the A button at the same time. Select save and then choose another character to play with. Watch those points soar!

Get Information

When you are in a town, use the A button to talk to natives. If you hit the B button when there is nobody around, a secret message sometimes will appear.

Know Your Magic

Do not enter a castle or its labyrinth unless you know some magic, or you are sure to die!

Defeat Carock

To beat this mighty guardian, you must have Reflect magic. Activate this magic, and then crouch low on the left edge of the screen. Be patient, and wait for him to fire at you, for his fire will bounce back and hurt him. Neat and easy!

Defeat Doomknocker

This tricky enemy is hard to beat. One hint is to attack from above by jumping off the ledges and onto his head. You must also use the Reflect magic.

The Fifth Palace

The only way to get to the fifth palace is by floating on the water with the winged boots. They are located in the Palace of Maze Island.

Get Past Locked Doors

You will often encounter a locked door and you will not have a key. This is no problem, though, if you have the Fairy spell, for when you have transformed into a fairy, you can fly right through keyholes.

Stay on the Paths

If you stay on the paths throughout the game, you will not have to bother fighting any enemies. They will appear, and look mean, but they will not attack you if you are on the paths.

Death Mountain Maze

While you are journeying through the maze in Death Mountain, remember this bit of advice: *always* travel to the *right,* never go left. When you finally reach the King's Graveyard, you will find the entrance to a cave that will bring you to the island.

Get the Hammer

There is a cave near Death Mountain that holds the hammer. You must have the hammer to play the game.

123

Turbo Tips

1943—*Mission Select*
To start your game on mission 8, use this code: *PFL08.* To start your game on mission 22, which is the third-to-last level of the game, use this code: *RY690.* To start your game on the next-to-last level—with a whole lot of powers—use this code: *TY19U.*

3-D WORLD RUNNER—*Continue*
After your game has ended, push UP and A at the same time.

ADVENTURE ISLAND—*See the Next Enemy*
After you have defeated the boss at the end of a level, his head will come off. Immediately press START, and the head of the next boss will appear on the defeated boss.

ARKANOID—*Secret Continue and Stage Select*
To continue a game at the start of the level you die on, hold down both the A and B buttons while pressing SELECT five times. Push START and you'll be on the same screen you died on. To start on a level between 1 and 16, hold down both the A and B buttons and press SELECT five times. Then press START to choose your level.

ARKANOID—*Stage Skip and Continue*
To skip a stage, push A, B, and START all at the same time. For stage skipping, follow this last instruction at the beginning of each level while the music is playing.

BASES LOADED—*Warp to Game 80!*
This passcode brings you to the championship game: *DNBHJGH.* Win it for a very exciting ending.

BIONIC COMMANDO—*Secret Escape*
Anytime during the game, you can magically warp out of the level you're on by pressing START, A, and B all at the same time.

BLASTER MASTER—*Defeat 4th-Stage Boss*
This giant frog has three methods of attack: He shoots out his tongue, he spits fireballs everywhere, and he throws one large ball of fire. An easy way to beat him is to position yourself to his left, your gun towards his open mouth, and wait until he spits out his tongue. Fire!

BLASTER MASTER—*Defeat the Brain*
Use grenades to kill the big Brain. Stay close to it but keep moving around to avoid its murderous cells.

BLASTER MASTER—*Mega Weapons*
When you press DOWN and B, your homing missile destroys close enemies, even if they are hiding. Use your thunder break and multiwarhead missile in the same way to destroy other enemies.

BLASTER MASTER—*Rover Power Up*
To boost the power level of your Rover, you must defeat a Warlord.

BUBBLE BOBBLE—*Pick Your Level*
EECJJ is the code for level 112, and *EECFG* is the code for level 112 in SUPER BUBBLE BOBBLE. After you enter one of these codes, you can pick *any level* by pressing the A and B buttons. Cool! Rad!

BUMP 'N' JUMP—*Bonus and Continue*
If you die and want to continue your game on the last level you were on, just do this at the end of your game: While holding SELECT on controller 1, press A and B at the same time on controller 2. Then press START twice on controller 1.

To get 50,000 points as a bonus, all you have to do is stay away from all of the cars. If you get through the level without touching any of the other cars, you will be fabulously rewarded.

BUMP 'N JUMP—*Secret Continue*
Right after your game is over, hold down the SELECT button on controller 1 while pushing the A and B buttons on controller 2 at the same time. Then push START twice on controller 2.

COMMANDO—*Secret Ladder Seeing Glasses*
To play the game so that all of the secret rooms and stairways are already shown on the screen (and no bombing is necessary), on controller 2, press LEFT, LEFT, LEFT, B, B, A, A, A, A, and finally, press START on controller 1. Rad!

CONTRA—*30 Free Men*
On the player select screen, quickly press UP, UP, DOWN, DOWN, LEFT, RIGHT, LEFT, RIGHT, B, A, START. This trick will give you 30 extra men, and after they are all used, and you continue, you will be given 30 *more* men.

DEADLY TOWERS—*Mega Weapons Password*
After you enter this password—*54DKDKYISB*—go into the second door on the right outside the castle and go up the tower to the big boss.

DEADLY TOWERS—*Mega Powers*
To make Prince Meyer have all of the possible hit points, defenses, and attack weapons, start the game and let yourself be killed as quickly as possible. Change the first two digits of your password to *FE* and punch in this revised password.

DR. CHAOS—*End Code*
If you use this code—*WPJSO2SG 6VK6CH77L*—you will not only be warped to the last stage of this game, but you will also be equipped with all of the items that you could possibly hold.

FLYING DRAGON—*Championship Match Code*
To warp yourself right to the last fight of the game, use this passkey: *B A A A.*

GHOSTS AND GOBLINS—*Secret Stage Choice*
To choose which level you start on, do this on the title screen: Hold the controller to the right while you press B three times in a row. Then press UP, B, B, B, LEFT, B, B, B, DOWN, B, B, B, and finally START.

GOONIES 2—*Mega Password*
This passcode will start you off with a character that has all the secret items and has saved all six Goonies: *Y" " ↓ 'U'S"3"CR.*

GUN.SMOKE—*Mega Weapons*
At the title screen, press A, A, A, A, SELECT, SELECT, SELECT, SELECT, RIGHT, RIGHT, START. *Wowee!* Look at those weapons!

GYRUSS—*30 Extra Ships!*
To get your 30 free ships, press A, B, RIGHT, LEFT, RIGHT, LEFT, DOWN, DOWN, DOWN, UP, UP and then START on controller 1.

HACKER 2—*Security Code*
If you get the security code, you will get it in four pieces. Rearrange the four pieces to form an *important date in American history.*

HOOPS—*Game 28 Code*
WOW! Start two games away from winning the series against the computer by using this code: *PPCQXCRCY.*

ICE HOCKEY—*Lose the Goalies*
Hold down the A and B buttons on both controllers at the same time and press START on controller 1 to be rid of those annoying goalies.

IKARI WARRIORS—*Secret Continue*
To continue from exactly the same point that you died on, press A, B, B, A. Cool!

IKARI WARRIORS—*Stage Select*
On the title screen push UP, DOWN, A, A, B, LEFT, RIGHT, A, B, UP, A, DOWN, RIGHT, RIGHT, LEFT, B, UP,

LEFT, A, RIGHT, B, LEFT, RIGHT, A, LEFT, UP, A, DOWN, A, RIGHT, LEFT, A, START. Next to the airplane crash-landing screen, stage 1 will appear. Press the A button to select your stage. You have to be fast, though.

IKARI WARRIORS 2: *Victory Road*
The A, B, B, A Continue method is the same as in Ikari 1. However, it will not work in your final battle against Zang Zip.

IRON TANK—*Secret Pass Codes*
To start the game at pretty high areas, such as right outside the enemies headquarters, punch in these two codes: *6276064* and *2110944*.

JACKAL—*The End*
At the end of the sixth stage, you will see an elevated tower. Hit it directly in the center with your explosives and a tank will appear. Dodge its fire and hit it with your explosives to wear it down.

KARNOV—*Level Select*
On the title screen, hold down SELECT, A, and B and push RIGHT on controller 1. *At the same time* on controller 2, press the A button once to start on level 2, twice to start on level 3, etc. When you have chosen the level, press START.

KID NIKI—*Secret Bonus Stage*
At the beginning of round 4, go to the left and position yourself at the end of the cliff. Hold DOWN for about 4 or 5 seconds. You will flash and then disappear and be warped into a room with four eggs. Open all of them to find important and useful items.

KUNG-FU HERO—*Secret Continue*
After your game ends and you see the title screen, hold down the A button while pressing START. You'll continue from the exact place where you died.

LABYRINTH—*Key Substitute*
When you get to a place where you need a key, but have only a plank, use the plank instead. It will do fine as a substitute.

MAG MAX—*Secret Robot Parts*
To get the parts to your Mag-Max robot to fit together earlier in the game, try shooting the grey house that appears once in a while. Although the house is said to be invincible, you can blow it up and you'll be rewarded with a robot part. If you already have all your robot parts, you'll receive 1,000 bonus points.

MEGA MAN 2—*Baby Bird Stars*
To change the stars (shown with the boss at the beginning of each round) into little baby birds, press both the A and B buttons while holding the control pad in the direction of the boss.

MEGA MAN—*Multiple Shots*
Use this trick on the One-Eyed Rock Monster—or any other monster, for that matter. Use the Elecman beam to fire a shot at him, and just as it hits him, start pressing the SELECT button over and over again. This will pause the game many times, and it will injure the enemy each time!

MIKE TYSON'S PUNCH OUT!!—*Another World Circuit*
To get to "Another World Circuit," put in this code: *135 792 4680*. Also try this other code to see the names of the people who made the game: *106 113 0120*. After you punch in the code, you must hold down the SELECT button while holding A and B.

PREDATOR—*The Final Conflict*
At the end of the game, you must pull the rope in order to make the log drop on the last enemy.

PROPHECY—*The Capital Clue*
When you talk to a priest and he gives you a message which has the first letter of each word CAPITALIZED, put those capital letters together for a clue. Also, when you get to the Water Shrine, be sure to draw a map for yourself, since the way can get pretty confusing.

Q*BERT—*Infinite Continues*
To get unlimited Continues, press UP and SELECT on controller 1, and DOWN and B on controller 2. Then on controller 2 press LEFT, then RIGHT.

RACKET ATTACK—*Final Match Code*
To start on the last match against the computer, use this code: *BPDHEFB.*

RAMBO—*End of the Game*
To begin your game at the end of the game, use this code: *yDaB pc71 jQOA uT3D nfWW 3UKT Yv4g G5WH.* Phew! After all that punching in, you had better have typed the letters correctly!

RENEGADE—*Stage Select*
To warp to stage 2 at the start of any mission, hold DOWN on controller 2 while pressing DOWN, UP, RIGHT, UP, LEFT, UP, and then START on controller 2. For stage 3, hold DOWN on controller 1 while pressing UP, DOWN, LEFT, DOWN, RIGHT, DOWN, then START on controller 1. For stage 4, press DOWN, DOWN, UP, UP, RIGHT, LEFT, then START on controller 1 while holding UP on controller 2.

SEICROSS—*Continue and Invincibility*
For a Continue, hold the A button down while you press START on the Game Over screen. To make yourself invincible, hold the A and B buttons on controller 2 while pressing LEFT and on controller 1, press UP, UP, DOWN, DOWN, then START. Neato!

SEICROSS—*Double Your Bonus*
At the end of each stage, when all the blue men are lined up on the top of the screen, move your ship over and *save them again!* This also gives you 1,000 points for each man again.

SEICROSS—*Warp*
To warp to a harder level, hold A and B and push LEFT on controller 2 and select the level you want with controller 1.

SKY KID—*Secret Continue*
To continue your game on the last level you were on, press to the lower-left diagonal on controller 2 and press START on controller 1. Easy!

SOLOMAN'S KEY—*Secret Bonus and Game Switch*
On your first man, when you get to the 17th level and hit the unbreakable grey block on the far right 11 times in a row, your Dana character will be changed into the good ole' Mighty Bomb Jack. Also, all of the characters on the screen will turn into bonus-holding fairies.

SPY HUNTER—*Get a Loaded Car*
On the title screen, hold the SELECT button and A and B and push in the middle of the control pad. Push START and you will have a car with oil slick, smoke screen, and missiles.

SPY HUNTER—*Mega Weapons*
To start your game with all of the possible weapons and 10 extra men, hold A, B, SELECT, and RIGHT at the same time. Then press START.

SUPER PITFALL—*Secret Continue*
To continue your last game, press A, A, A, SELECT, SELECT, and START when you are at the title screen.

TEMCO BOWL—*Super Bowl!*
To start off the season with the Super Bowl, use this code: *9L7FBFA5.*

THE LAST NINJA 2—*The Final Conflict*
At the end of the game, you must punch in the combination that you got from the computer earlier in the game. Then you must light all of the candles and kill the enemy in the center of the screen. If you do not act fast, he will blow out some of your candles.

THE LEGEND OF ZELDA—*2nd Quest*
To start off in the 2nd quest, type ZELDA instead of your own name.

TIGER HELI—*Secret Continue*
As in Ikari Warriors, when you die you can continue right there. It is easier to do in Tiger Heli, though, because all you have to do is press the A and B buttons at the same time.

TMNT—*Pizza*
Most pizzas are hidden in the action screens. The action scenes are down manholes in Area 1.

TMNT—*Turtle Power*
If the turtle you are using is getting weak, switch to a stronger one. When you get a slice of pizza, remember to feed it to the weaker turtles.

TRACK AND FIELD 2—*Hammer Throw Record*
Make sure that your power is either at the 0 or
a lower level in "POWER" and start spinning the
hammer in a counterclockwise direction. When your
man starts to flash, hold down the A button and
release it when the angle makes a V (about 80°). Even
though the hammer won't go very far, you will make
the new World Record with a whopping 92.04 meters!

TROJAN—*Secret Continue*
To continue from where you last left off, push UP
and START at the same time.

ZANAC—*Mega Ship and 1-UP*
To make your ship a super plane, press and hold A
and B while pressing START on the title screen. Once
you get your 6th powerup, you will have a 1-UP
party—everything you see will transform into a 1-UP!

ZANAC—*Secret Continue and Stage Select*
While you are in the Continue mode, hold UP and
push the A button. This trick is helpful when you
get to a level higher than 10, because the regular
Continue mode doesn't go any higher. To choose the
stage, press RESET on the console 13 times and then
press START. By pressing LEFT or RIGHT, you can select
from stages 1 through 10.

123

Mini Tips and Game Summaries

BAD DUDES *(by Data East)*
You can choose to play with one player or to play against your friend. Blade and Striker are the dudes you control while trying to get the Dragon Ninja gang. This gang has captured the President, and your job is to find him.

BASES LOADED *(by Jaleco)*
This is probably the most realistic baseball video game made for Nintendo. There are nine ways to swing the bat and lots of different pitches to throw. When you pick a team, you get to choose your lineup from 30 players. Another option is to choose Pennant. When you do, you start a 132-game season against the computer, and it keeps a record of your wins and losses. Hint: Try beaning the cleanup batter or whoever is the best hitter on the other team— Fight! Fight!

BLADES OF STEEL *(by Konami)*
Awesome graphics and realistic hockey play make this game a good one. The violence of real ice hockey is brought to life in this game cartridge. If you get mad at another player and hit him, a brawl immediately breaks out. A new screen appears with a closeup of the fight: Your sticks go down and the fight begins! Whether you win or lose, you'll both have to sit in the penalty box for a while. This feature adds that extra *boom* to this game.

BREAKTHRU *(by Data East)*
You must drive through five areas occupied by enemy forces to rescue a top-secret airplane that was stolen. Along the way you will meet up with enemies while you are piloting helicopters, driving bulletproof cars, and dodging hidden snipers. When crossing the mountains, you will be set back by rockslides. Every so often, a power barrel will parachute down from the sky to boost your bullets.

CITY CONNECTION *(by Jaleco)*

You are a burglar who has just stolen a big load of paint; it is dripping out of the back of your car and marking your path behind you. You must escape from the police of New York, Paris, Frankfurt, London, Tokyo, and New Delhi to win the game. To pass a level, you must successfully drip paint onto the entire freeway, without running over a stray cat. HINT: Pick up oil cans and shoot them at police cars to make the COPS crash.

COBRA COMMAND *(by Data East)*

While flying your heavily armoured helicopter through six stages, you must destroy enemy tanks, cannons, subs, and gunboats. You must rescue hostages during the night, over the China Sea, and on the mountains. Pressing the SELECT button during play lets you choose to send a ladder down to someone, use better armour, or different missiles. There is even a Continue mode.

CONTRA *(by Konami)*

Two buff soldiers, Scorpion and Mad Dog, must fight their way through army bases, snow fields, jungles, and waterfalls to get to the evil Red Falcon. To kill him, you must get to the last level, the Dragon's Lair and blow up his heart, causing a chain reaction that blows up the whole island.

This game is fun and addictive, and is virtually impossible with only three men. To get thirty (30!) men, punch in this sequence on controller 1 at the title screen: UP, UP, DOWN, DOWN, LEFT, RIGHT, LEFT, RIGHT, B, A, (SELECT), START. Pressing SELECT is optional. Use it only for a two-player game. Have Fun!

DOUBLE DRAGON *(by Tradewest)*

Billy and Jimmy have set out to rescue Billy's girl-friend who has been kidnapped by the Black Warriors gang. En route to finding the leader, Shadow Boss,

Billy and Jimmy must use a combination of 11 karate moves and pick up enemy weapons like baseball bats, whips, and barrels in order to kill enemies.

DOUBLE DRIBBLE *(by Konami)*
This is best known for its slow-motion super graphics dunk screen. When you go in for a dunk, and you hold down the B button until the last possible second, the fan-filled bleachers and the enlarged picture of a man in the air slamming the ball into the hoop appear, accompanied by the sound of a gun shot. On the Mode Select screen, you can choose to be one of four teams, play at one of three skill levels, and choose how long the quarters are. There are even free throws for fouls. If you choose to play against the computer and you win, you get a giant trophy at the end. Sasha Peterson is the absolute master at this game—no doubt about it!

GUN.SMOKE *(by Capcom)*
You play Marshal Billy Bob as he tries to kill all the bad guys in Hicksville. You are a trigger-happy cowboy lookin' for a showdown. Your enemies have dynamite, knives, and shotguns, but as you advance to harder levels, you become armed with magnums, napalm, and machine guns.

GYRUSS *(by Ultra)*
The object of this game is to save the universe from the Gyrusian monsters. You must save all the people living throughout the solar system and fly through the stars to do it. It is a fast-paced game that will increase your blood pressure.

ICE HOCKEY *(by Nintendo)*
This is an extremely fast action game (unless you set it for a really slow speed). You can choose your team, the speed of play, and you even choose the size of your players. Small players can burn across the ice. Medium men are kind of average—they can go fairly fast and can hit the puck pretty hard. Big fat guys move like army tanks, and fire like them too! Hint: If

you hold down the "fire" button for a second or two and then release, the puck will zip across the ice at a high speed, and actually lift off the ice.

JACKAL *(by Konami)*
You must complete six levels of action freeing prisoners in your jeep, armed with a machine gun and grenades. When you free a P.O.W. in Vietnam, you must hurry him to a convenient helicopter landing pad. The more prisoners you free, the bigger chance you have of earning bazookas or even extra jeeps. Hint: Blow up hidden stars, which are usually located in the corners of the screen, to kill all the enemies on the screen at once.

KARATE CHAMP *(by Data East)*
This is a one-on-one karate competition game, where you can do kicks, spins, somersaults, lunges, blocks, footsweeps, and punches. There are three bonus screens, and on one of them, you get to fight a charging bull! You must be fast and have good reflexes to master all nine different settings of matches.

KID NIKI: RADICAL NINJA *(by Data East)*
You must go through seven bosses before the little karate expert Kid Niki can defeat the Stone Wizard. He is on a mission to rescue Princess Margo, and he will do anything and everything he must do to save her. He only has the Spinning Sword, but Niki must rescue his girl.

LEE TRAVINO'S FIGHTING GOLF *(by SNK)*
Select to golf either on an American course or a Japanese course, your player and clubs, and get ready to spend a day at the country club! Pretty Amy, Big Jumbo, Super Mex, and Miracle Chosuke are the golfers you can choose among at the beginning of the game. They each have different strengths and weaknesses. Also, try the practice mode to boost your skill level. Have fun!

LEGENDARY WINGS *(by Capcom)*

This game takes place 20,000 years in the future, when the world is ruled by a mega computer called Dark. When Dark malfunctions, robot warships and monsters come from nowhere to guard Dark's underground base. You play the role of a superpowered winged fighter that must kill all the monsters. The Giant Head, which guards Dark's base, will suck you into its mouth if you get too close. Hint: Try to destroy all of the targets on the ground, because in some of them lies a secret whirlpool that warps you to a bonus stage.

MAJOR LEAGUE BASEBALL *(by LJN)*

You can choose your team from a list of 26 teams in the beginning of this game. There are three different games to choose from: a World Series game, an All-Star game, or a regular season game. You can even check the stamina of your players during the game.

MIKE TYSON'S PUNCH OUT! *(by Nintendo)*

Little Mac, played by you, is out to fight the world until he reaches the dream fight against World Champion, Mike Tyson. Mac can throw five different punches and dodge attacks from two directions. If you land a good hard punch at the right time, you receive an uppercut star, but be careful, because the second you get hit by your opponent, you lose that uppercut. Between rounds you talk to your trainer and if you get hurt, he rubs your shoulder. Hint: Press the SELECT button when your trainer is talking to you to refill your energy. If you press SELECT before the first round, you will *lose* half your energy. Super Hint: Use this code—*007 373 5963*—to fight Mike Tyson.

PRO WRESTLING *(by Nintendo)*

You can choose from six macho wrestlers, each with different moves. For example, one of the men can do the "pirhana bite," and another specializes in "back breakers." You can even head-butt sometimes. Hint: Throw your opponent over the ropes, out of the ring.

If you can keep him down there for 20 seconds, and you can get yourself back into the ring, you are the winner!

R.B.I. BASEBALL *(by Tengen)*
You're probably getting sick of baseball games by now, so this is the last one. We like R.B.I. for its three-way screen splitting. When you are at bat, you can see the batter and pitcher, first base and its runner, and third base and its runner—all in separate cuts of the screen! You use real players' names and stats, and fireworks go off in the sky when you bash a homerun.

RACKET ATTACK *(by Jaleco)*
This is an extremely realistic version of tennis. You can select one of eight men or women, and choose to play on a clay, concrete, or even a grass court. The sound effects are awesome, including the umpire calls, and the screaming crowds. Serve, run up to the net, and put the ball away to end the match. This game has got some pretty awesome reviews, especially from buddy, "Yiddew Dougwas."

ROLLERBALL *(by Hal America)*
If you like pinball, you'll love Rollerball. Flashing lights and sound effects make it fun to play. The screen shows an extremely detailed pinball machine. Also included in the Game Pak is a cross between pinball and hockey, for two players. The object is to score goals by hitting the puck-ball with your flippers.

SKATE OR DIE *(by Ultra)*
This has a whole bunch of events to choose from, ranging from ramps and downhill races to tricks and even a violent joust at the end where you try to knock the other person off his board with a pole. The game is pretty good fun, but it is easily mastered, so it gets boring after a while. Hint: Jump on the hood of the police car to get a bonus.

TRACK AND FIELD 2 *(by Konami)*
You can choose from 15 events, including archery, fencing, gymnastics, swimming, or pole vaulting. You can choose to play against the computer or a friend. The graphics are pretty good, and the action is raw.

WINTER GAMES *(by Acclaim)*
In this game, you play four different Winter-Olympic type games: Bobsledding, Speed Skating, Hot Dog (the best), and Figure Skating. The graphics are hot, and so is the action. Sorry—no hints!

WOOD AND WATER RAGE *(by LJN)*
This is a California surfing and skateboarding game. While hittin' the waves, you can do a number of hot tricks, including spinouts, "Hanging Ten," and "Riding the Pipeline." In the skating part of the game, you have to earn points by doing tricks. Dodging turtles, guardrails, and small cars earns you points, as do jumps off ramps among other tricks. Surf or die, dude!